TITLE II - A

PARETO'S GENERAL SOCIOLOGY
A PHYSIOLOGIST'S INTERPRETATION

PARETO'S
GENERAL SOCIOLOGY
A PHYSIOLOGIST'S INTERPRETATION

BY

LAWRENCE J. HENDERSON
HARVARD UNIVERSITY

NEW YORK / RUSSELL & RUSSELL

PREFACE

THE subject of the present Essay is the sociological work of Vilfredo Pareto, by birth an Italian Marquis, by education and profession an engineer, who had become professor of economics in the University of Lausanne. This work was first published in 1916 under the title *Trattato di Sociologia Generale*.

Books are rare that derive from such wide and varied experience as Pareto's, and those are rarer still that utilize such experience so completely. There is hardly an important element in the life of the author that has not left its mark upon the book. He was born of a French mother in 1848 at Paris, schooled in France, and professionally educated in Italy. His birth and natural endowments assured him a wide experience of everyday affairs, and must have aided in the attainment of intellectual detachment. His education afforded both a broad classical culture and training in mathematics and in physical science. He practiced engineering in Tuscany for two decades and meanwhile dabbled in Italian politics, took part in the social life of Florence, and read widely. Then he attacked mathematical economics as a serious study. In 1893, at the age of forty-five, he was elected to the chair of economics at Lausanne, and a period of

61993

fruitful activity as an economist followed. About ten years later, turning his diverse experiences to good account, he began the systematic study of sociology. This soon became his chief occupation, and so remained to the end of his life. He died at Céligny in 1923.

I have found pleasure and profit in the careful study of the *Treatise on General Sociology*. As my familiarity with the work has increased, I have become convinced that acquaintance with Pareto's analysis of facts, with his synthesis of results, with his methods, and with some of his theorems is at present indispensable for the interpretation of a wide range of phenomena, whenever and wherever men act and react upon one another. Meanwhile, I have come to see, or to believe that I see, how and why it is difficult for those who have had little experience with the natural sciences to understand the Treatise. So far as I am aware of my motives in writing the present Essay, they are indicated well enough by these few remarks.

I have tried hard to be brief, to be orderly, and to achieve that measure of unity of which the material admits. But the Treatise is long; though orderly, it is extremely complex, and it contains an extraordinary and bewildering variety of facts and considerations. Therefore the task has been difficult and I fear that my success is but imperfect. Such as it is, it depends upon relegating the discussion of several topics to the notes. But some of the notes are indispensable as justifications of bald assertions of the Essay. Other notes are intended to clear up particular topics.

In the last paragraph of the Essay, I have said that Pareto's Treatise bears all the marks of the spade-work of a pioneer. I would particularly emphasize the fact that it is a first approximation, and beg the reader to keep this in mind always, but not to forget the important qualification that Pareto makes effective use throughout the book of his intimate acquaintance with some of the most highly developed sciences.

I am much indebted to Mr. Henry Seidel Canby, who has kindly consented to the incorporation in this Essay of my brief review of Pareto's Treatise, recently published in the Saturday Review of Literature.

L. J. H.

CAMBRIDGE, MASSACHUSETTS

CONTENTS

PARETO'S GENERAL SOCIOLOGY

I

INTRODUCTION

THE ancient religion "was one of the chief causes of the prosperity of Rome; for this religion gave rise to well regulated conduct, and such conduct brings good fortune, and from good fortune results the happy success of undertakings." [1] So four centuries ago wrote a modern thinker, setting down in judicious phrases the influence of the sentiments upon the actions of men, and consequently upon the fate of principalities and republics. Time has dealt variously with Machiavelli and with his writings. The character and motives of the man have been little praised and greatly blamed by those numerous persons who could not or would not confine themselves to relevant criticism of his work; but this work, which was scientific before the birth of modern science, has on the whole withstood criticism. Long ago Bacon declared, "We are much beholden to Machiavel and others that write what men do and not what they ought to do."

In order to fix our ideas, it will be convenient to take an example and to note some of its particular

[1] Machiavelli, *Discourses on the First Decade of Titus Livy*, Book I, Chap. XI.

aspects. In Chapter XVIII of *The Prince*, Machiavelli says, "Everyone admits how praiseworthy it
is in a prince to keep faith, and to live with integrity and not with craft. Nevertheless, our experience has been that those princes who have done
great things have held good faith of little account,
and have known how to circumvent the intellect of
men by craft, and in the end have overcome those
who have relied on their word." On this text the
following remarks and queries may be set down at
random:

(1) In reading this and similar passages most
people feel disgust or horror, much as they do in
reading descriptions of certain diseases, and fail to
notice objectively the character of what they have
read.

(2) They often transfer their dislike from the
book to the author.

(3) Thus both book and author have acquired a
bad name and it has become difficult for anyone to
approach the book dispassionately.

(4) Machiavelli's statement is an induction from
experience.

(5) Is this induction well founded? Is it con-
firmed by later experience with later forms of
society? One thinks of such instances as the careers
of Henri IV of France, of Elizabeth of England, of
Frederic II of Prussia who wrote the *Anti-Mach-
iavel*, of Napoleon, and, as political conditions

change, of the foremost modern ministers, such as Richelieu, Walpole, Bismarck, and Cavour, — but perhaps without reaching a firm conclusion.

(6) Does this induction hold for the heads of other forms of government?

(7) What are the limitations on the 'great things' which depend upon the condition that they shall be done in this way and by such princes?

(8) Is the publication of similar inductions useful to society?

(9) Are the sentiments that find expression in the widespread dislike of Machiavelli useful to society?

(10) Why have social scientists not followed Machiavelli's example? In what manner and how far have they been influenced by their own sentiments and interests, by the sentiments of others, and by 'public opinion'?

(11) What preparations and precautions are likely to make for similar successes or similar failures in the investigation of similar questions?

(12) What were Machiavelli's sentiments and motives? But the answer to this question is of infinitesimal scientific importance.[1]

(13) Even after we have considered these points, I think we all find that our own sentiments still make it very difficult to estimate the correctness of Machiavelli's induction.

[1] See note 1 below, p. 63.

(14) Most of these remarks and queries bear upon important general problems of sociology.

Into such considerations we may now try to introduce some small measure of definition and order, proceeding slowly, step by step.

II

SOCIAL SCIENCE AND NATURAL SCIENCE

MACHIAVELLI's work endures, but has engendered little of like quality or substance, and until the publication in 1916 of the *Trattato di Sociologia Generale* [1] by Vilfredo Pareto there had been very little further advance in scientific description and logical analysis of the influence of the sentiments upon human affairs.[2]

Three hundred years ago Galileo was writing his *Dialogues Concerning Two New Sciences*, one of the few books that bear, like Machiavelli's, the mark of the highest originality. Unlike Machiavelli, Galileo helped to set in motion an activity that has become one of the most important and influential in the world today. The fruits of Machiavelli's labors are few and uncertain, those of Galileo's are countless and unmistakable. Why? Partly, we may be sure, because the two great Florentines studied different subjects.

[1] *Trattato di Sociologia Generale*, 2 vols., Firenze, Barbera, 1916. Definitive edition, 3 vols., Firenze, Barbera, 1923. *Traité de Sociologie Générale*, 2 vols., Lausanne and Paris, Payot, 1917, 1918. *The Mind and Society*, 4 vols., New York, Harcourt, Brace & Company, 1935.

[2] See note 2 below, p. 69.

It will be well, for this reason, to glance at all knowledge.

The endless catalogue of words that designate the subjects taught in our universities seems to defy rational classification. Nevertheless, I think that many of these subjects may be reasonably divided into two classes, thus:

First: history, literature, economics, sociology, law, politics, theology, education, etc.

Second: logic, mathematics, physics, biology and other natural sciences, grammar, harmony, etc.

The importance of some such dichotomy is indeed widely felt, and gives rise to much discussion and to heated controversies.

Let us look at the facts dispassionately. When the adepts of subjects of the second class disagree, it is a peculiarity of their behavior that they do so most often at the frontiers of knowledge, where growth is taking place; and in the long run a debated question is ordinarily settled by observation, experiment, or some other method that all accept. This is by no means true in many, and hardly true in any, of the subjects of the first class. (Of course, it is true in parts of these subjects.) Now this remarkable difference between the behavior of students of the two classes of subjects is probably related to a difference in subject matter. For all the subjects of the first class do involve, and none of the subjects of the second class does involve, the study of the interrelations of two or more persons.

We are now in a position to approach by way of another science and then to consider the central feature of Pareto's Sociology.

III

THE PHYSICO–CHEMICAL SYSTEM

AN IMPORTANT characteristic of many of the natural sciences is the concept of a system, for example, the solar system. In order to fix our ideas, we may consider Willard Gibbs's generalized description of a physico-chemical system, which is the basis of a famous contribution [1] to theoretical science that has stood the test of a half century of criticism and use. A physico-chemical system is an isolated material aggregate. It consists of components, which are individual substances, like water or alcohol. These substances are found, singly or together, in phases. Phases are physically homogeneous solid, liquid, or gaseous parts of the system: for example, ice, or a solution of alcohol in water, or air. The system is further characterized by the concentrations of the components in the phases, by its temperature, and by its pressure.

The reader should note that this description of Gibbs's physico-chemical system is too brief to be rigorous. In particular, a more careful statement of the nature of components and more precise ter-

---

[1] The Scientific Papers of J. Willard Gibbs, Vol. I, *Thermodynamics*, London and New York, 1906, pp. 55–353.

minology with reference to concentrations are necessary for precision.

As an example of such a system, we may take a mixture of ice, soda-water, and whiskey in a tightly stoppered thermos bottle. Here the walls of the bottle afford some measure of isolation. In a first rough approximation, the components may be chosen as water, alcohol, and carbon dioxide, for the other constituents of whiskey and the oxygen and nitrogen of the air are physically and chemically of secondary importance. There are three phases: a solid phase, ice, made up of the component water in a nearly pure state, a liquid phase, and a gas phase. Both the liquid phase and the gas phase contain all three components, but in different concentrations. If the concentration of alcohol in the liquid phase is determined, or still better the concentrations of both alcohol and carbon dioxide, the temperature of the system is likewise determined. The pressure varies with the concentrations of the different components; it also varies with the temperature. Indeed variation in the concentration of any component or variation of pressure or of temperature is accompanied by variations in all other factors. For instance, if the pressure is increased within the system, as it may be by thrusting the stopper more deeply into the neck of the bottle, there will be a movement of substances from the gas phase to the liquid phase. In this manner the concentrations in both liquid and gas phases will be modified. There will also be a change of temperature, corresponding to the change of concentrations (compare freezing mixtures of ice and salt), and this will be accompanied by a change in the density, or concentration, of the solid phase. Thus all the factors that characterize this system are seen to be mutually dependent. In this respect this system is typical of all systems.

The complications that result from the state of interdependence of the variables present a logical problem of the first importance. It has arisen again and again in every science that has reached a certain stage of development, whenever the task of describing complex systems has presented itself and has been seriously attacked, and it has been invariably solved in accordance with the same principles. The essential feature of the situation may perhaps be set forth most clearly by noting that, in the present instance, the change of pressure, with which we set out, has been followed by a change of temperature. Now, if we permit ourselves to think in a chain of cause and effect relations, we are forced into the following position: It is evident that this change of temperature must result in a secondary change of pressure. Then, in turn, this secondary change of pressure must be followed by a secondary change of temperature, which again will lead to another modification of pressure, and so on in an infinite succession of approximations to a condition of equilibrium. All this is manifestly absurd, for on the one hand the readjustment of a disturbed equilibrium does not in fact proceed as if it were imitating a series of awkwardly calculated successive approximations (unless the process happens actually to go on by successive action and reaction); thus our analysis does not fit the facts. And on the other hand, this way of thinking is confusing, in a manner that cannot be tolerated in scientific analysis. In short, our conceptual scheme does not work. So it comes about that in such cases cause and effect analysis has to be replaced by some method of analysis involving the simultaneous variations of mutually dependent variables.[1] The classical example of this kind of analysis may be found in Lagrange's *Mécanique Analytique*, where the logical problem is solved in its most general form.

A clear understanding of the nature of mutual dependence is so necessary to the student of Pareto's work that I shall here add a simple mechanical example which I have already used elsewhere.[2]

Consider figure 1. The four rigid bodies A, B, C, and D are fastened to a framework a, b, c, d by the elastic bands 1, 2, 3, 4, and 5. A, B, C, and D are joined one to

[1] See note 3 below, p. 74.
[2] L. J. Henderson, *An Approximate Definition of Fact*, University of California Publications in Philosophy, Vol. 14, 1932, pp. 183, 184.

another by the elastic bands 6, 7, 8, 9, and 10. Here the conditions of statical equilibrium can be worked out mathematically, or determined empirically by introducing spring-balances into the bonds 1, 2, . . . 10, and reading the balances.

Now imagine the point of attachment of 5 on the frame to be moving toward b, all other points of attach-

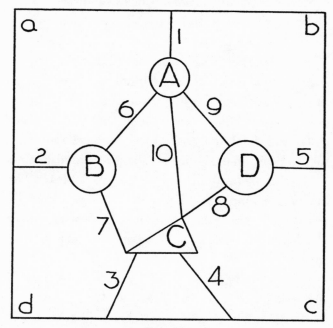

FIGURE 1

ment remaining unchanged. What will happen? Consider A. There will be action on A by the path 5, 9, by the path 5, 8, 10, and by the path 5, 8, 7, 6. But in each case these actions do not cease at A, just as they do not previously cease at D. The first, for example, continues along the path 10, 8, and so back to 5. If we try to think of all this as cause and effect we must inevitably reach a state of confusion.

Gibbs's system is plainly a fiction, for no real system can be isolated. Nevertheless, a close approach to isolation, as in a thermos bottle, is possible. So results are obtained and then extended even to systems that are far from isolated. Also, the enumeration of the factors, i.e. concentrations, temperature, and pressure, is incomplete. But it is ordinarily necessary to consider at least these three factors, and sometimes no more need be considered. In other cases the consideration of other factors, like those involved in capillary and electrical phenomena, cannot be avoided. Sometimes, however, such considerations may be introduced after the first analysis in the form of 'corrections.' Finally, the concept is often irrelevant; for instance, the consideration of a watch as a physico-chemical system would be a waste of time.

It need hardly be said that such apparent defects are in truth consequences of very real advantages. They are but signs of the well chosen simplifications and abstractions that make possible a systematic treatment of complex phenomena. This instrument that Gibbs has put in the chemists' service has immeasurably advanced the science of chemistry: it has clarified, directed, and economized the thought of all chemists. It enables us to understand, for example, refrigeration, the manufacture of steel, and the respiratory function of the blood.

IV

THE SOCIAL SYSTEM

THE central feature of Pareto's General Sociology is the construction of a similar conceptual scheme: the social system. This possesses many of the same logical advantages and limitations that are present in the physico-chemical system.[1] Pareto's social system contains individuals; they are roughly analogous to Gibbs's components. It is heterogeneous (cf. Gibbs's phases), for the individuals are of different families, trades, and professions; they are associated with different institutions and are members of different economic and social classes. As Gibbs considers temperature, pressure, and concentrations, so Pareto considers sentiments, or, strictly speaking, the manifestations of sentiments in words and deeds, verbal elaborations, and the economic interests. Like Gibbs, Pareto excludes many factors that are important in special cases, but he too has demonstrated that he can do much within the limitations that he has chosen, and that such limitations are necessary.

At this point I owe it to the reader to warn him that the analogies which I have pointed out are

[1] See note 4 below, p. 81.

accidental.[1] There is not the slightest reason to believe that Pareto was led to his theory by a consideration of the properties of a physico-chemical system. Also his work is in no sense an application of natural science to social science. But it is an application of the logical method that has been found useful [2] in all physical sciences and elsewhere when complex situations involving many variables in a state of mutual dependence are described. From long experience Pareto was intimately acquainted with the difficulties and constraints that arise in such an undertaking, and I think he was the first person thus equipped to attack the problem of sociology, and to make use of his equipment.

The parts and forces of the social system, like those of all analogous systems, are conceived as in a state of mutual dependence. They interact. Once again this arises from the fact that it is, in general,

[1] See note 5 below, p. 91.

[2] I.e., if I understand the term correctly, of the logical syntax that has been found useful. Cf. R. Carnap, *Logische Syntax der Sprache*, Wien, 1934, p. 207, "Wissenschaftslogik ist Syntax der Wissenschaftssprache," a proposition which, as elucidated by Carnap, amounts to something more than a definition.

For a much earlier discussion which gives explicitly or implicitly all that needs to be understood concerning this aspect of Pareto's method, see F. Y. Edgeworth, *Mathematical Psychics*, especially Appendix I, *On Unnumerical Mathematics*, London, 1881, or the 'Replika' reprint, London School of Economics and Political Science, London, 1932. In this work many of the criticisms of Pareto's *Treatise* that have been put forward by 'literary' sociologists were well answered fifty years ago.

impossible to explain the phenomena in terms of ordinary cause and effect. Therefore, such an explanation gives place to the type of description previously found necessary for dynamical, thermodynamical, physiological, and economic systems. So it comes about that the central feature of Pareto's use of his theory is the analysis of mutually dependent variations of his variables. In this difficult task he has been aided not only by mastery, resulting from his knowledge of mathematics, of the logical principles that are involved, but also by exceptional skill in diagnosis, and by wide learning and experience.

The social system thus defined and characterized is clearly an instrument that may be employed, within limits similar to those above explained for the physico-chemical system, in studying all the above-mentioned subjects of the first class. For, like history, literature, law, and theology, all these subjects are conversant with the interactions of individuals in their manifold relations, with their sentiments and interests, with their sayings and doings, while none can dispense with considerations of the mutual dependence of many factors. Pareto's Sociology, *in so far as it will bear the test of experience*, is thus seen to be applicable to all subjects of the first class. This is the ground for his choice of the title: "A Treatise on *General* Sociology." [1]

[1] See note 6 below, p. 93.

Some readers of this work are dissatisfied or confused because at the very outset Pareto refuses to set up a precise definition of the term *sociology*. He then points out that we have no rigorous definition of any science, that we can have none because we divide our knowledge into departments arbitrarily and for convenience, and that since our convenience changes with the increase of knowledge, our classification and delimitation of the sciences likewise changes. He might have added that while we remain within a field we are likely to find it unnecessary to perform logical operations that involve the field as a whole, and that so long as this is the case a rigorous definition of the field is, strictly speaking, useless.

After the preceding description of Pareto's system, it is, however, possible to make a further statement. *For the purposes of Pareto's book* social systems are concrete phenomena that may be considered, in a rough approximation, as falling within the class of phenomena defined by Pareto's generalized system, and sociology is, therefore, *for the purposes of the Treatise*, the analytical and synthetical study of these concrete phenomena. It is evident that, conformably with Pareto's above-mentioned remarks, this delimitation is arbitrary, that it is liable to modification in time, and that it is partly the result of restrictions imposed by Pareto for convenience.

V

ANALYSIS

THE social system makes its appearance on page 1308 [1] of Pareto's book.[2] It has been preceded by a painstaking choice, discrimination, description, and classification of its elements. The first quarter of the book, a study of the non-logical actions of men, leads up to the demonstration that no other elements of the social system are more important than the sentiments.[3] From this it is inferred that the sentiments must always be methodically considered (except in the rare cases when it can be proved that they may be neglected) in the study of any social system whatever. The task, however, is beset with difficulties, for we observe only manifestations of the sentiments, not the sentiments themselves. Indeed, the existence of the sentiments in a social system, like the existence of the forces in a dynamical system, is an assumption, a theory, or, in current phrase, a convention. Next, the sentiments often manifest themselves indistinctly; they are commonly enshrouded in words

[1] P. 1308 of the French edition.
[2] See note 7 below, p. 96.
[3] See note 8 below, p. 97.

and in non-logical reasoning; their manifestations occur not singly but in aggregates. Again, our own sentiments interfere with an unprejudiced analysis of the manifestations of the sentiments of others. In particular, students of the social sciences are commonly moved by their own sentiments, "whence proceed," as Bacon said, "sciences as one would." [1] And last, no sentiment is more troublesome than that which leads 'ideologists,' the 'intelligentsia' or 'intellectuals,' and in fact all of us, to mistake as rational what is non-rational in human behavior. This is perhaps the most important of the numerous reasons why Pareto was the first to make a taxonomic study of the manifestations of the sentiments. Meanwhile, a piece of work has been done in their allied but narrower quasi-pathological field by the psychoanalysts. For the present we may well look with suspicion upon psychoanalytical theories, but many facts are firmly established,[2] and they confirm this portion of Pareto's work.

[1] Novum Organum, Book I, Aphorism XLIX.

[2] The importance of not going beyond the *facts* of psychoanalysis— i.e. the reports of observed residues (complexes) and derivations (rationalizations) — may be illustrated by means of a statement of Freud's, *International Journal of Psycho-Analysis*, vol. XVII (1932), p. 405: "Now I conjecture that, in order to possess himself of fire, it was necessary for man to renounce the homosexually tinged desire to extinguish it with a stream of urine." Under the influence of his theory, which from a scientific standpoint is a vague working hypothesis, but which has become a residue for him just as it has for his disciples, the distinguished author fails to consider that the hypothetical desire

the derivations rapidly. For example, the instinct of conformity is a sentiment that is widely manifested as a residue. This is relatively constant. The endlessly varied actions that are involved in following the fashion and the no less varied explanations that accompany them and depend upon this and other residues (good taste, beauty, dignity, standing in the community, etc.) change rapidly. Such explanations are derivations.

The derivations may be considered as determined, in general and to a first approximation, by the residues. This is illustrated by a familiar phenomenon, involving what Pareto calls the logic of the sentiments, namely, the determination of the premises by the conclusion. For instance, a boy wishes to persuade his father to buy an automobile. He presents a reason; this is refuted as invalid; then another; this is shown to be inconsistent with the family's interests; then another which turns out to be incompatible with the father's sentiments; and so on until he succeeds, or abandons the attempt in despair or under compulsion. This is an example of one of the commonest forms of human behavior.

The actions of men are also in great part determined by the residues.[1] Accordingly the exhibition of the residues, no less than eating, drinking, or

---

[1] I.e. determined in the sense that, if the residues are known, something and in general much is thereby known about the actions.

breathing, may be recognized as a major function
of the human organism. It is therefore necessary
to take note that the role of the residues, or, speaking theoretically, of the sentiments that they manifest, is at least as important as the role of the logical
activities of men. Indeed nearly everything that is
accounted noblest and best, and also worst, in the
actions of men depends upon (i.e. is a function of)
residues. Vaguely recognized, this is no doubt one
of the most widely known rules of worldly wisdom.
What Pareto has done is to introduce a clear discrimination and a precise statement into a sys-
matic treatment of the complex phenomena, to
separate the residues from both logical and pseudo-
logical elaborations, to demonstrate that they are
of the first importance in the social system, and, in
particular, that their importance is in no way
diminished, but rather increased, by their inde-
pendence of logic.

Judging by the evidence, it appears that the
residues have ordinarily preceded the derivations
in the historical sequence. The residues of religion
have often preceded the derivations of theology;
the residues of justice, personal integrity, the welfare of the community, etc. have sometimes preceded the formation of these abstractions or the
formulation of laws and of legal concepts and fic-
tions, and in like manner customary law, which
sometimes found its first expression in rationalized

precepts, in rules of conduct, or in common law, was later codified in statutes. The residues concerning responsibility to the family and the community, of justice, of morality, of kindness and fair play, preceded these abstractions and the systematic derivations of ethics; many of them, indeed, occur in the actions of animals of widely different species where all verbal concepts seem to be absent.

The conclusions just stated do not agree with the common opinion, though lately, as a result of progress in anthropology and psychology, there are signs that this opinion is changing, and even in the past the nature of the phenomenon has been occasionally recognized by a clear thinker. Thus, in the preface to the *Laocoön* Lessing remarks, "Systematic books we Germans by no means lack, and we understand as well as any nation in the world how to deduce everything we wish in the most beautiful order from a few accepted explanations of words." This practice is by no means confined to Germans, but even those who have failed to reach Lessing's diagnosis have often noted its exceptional frequency among the Germans. A recent instance is Spengler's *Der Untergang das Abendlandes*. In Lessing's careful phrases, and in other instances that might be cited, the nature of systematic derivations is made clear, their worthlessness for the advancement of science is directly suggested, and their small social importance is implied. But, as Pareto shows, the history of systematic derivations remains a favorite subject with 'intellectuals,' and there are many for whom the history of political theories is the best part of political history, the history of theologies, the best part of the history of religions, and the history of thought, the best part of history. Some go even further and, erecting their own derivations into absolute principles of politics, of theology, or of metaphysics, treat the history of politics, of religions, or even all history as the history of pathological deviations from an imaginary normal state.

Even the most temperate and judicious students of history and the social sciences hardly ever consistently avoid the traditional assumption that the actions of men are logical. So, under the influence of the desire for logical explanations, and of the inveterate habit of making such explanations, which is perhaps one of the most uniform traits of educated men, they unconsciously neglect a question that should always be considered at the outset of an inquiry: Is a certain action logical or non-logical? Thus, in spite of the rapidly increasing scientific knowledge of the influence upon the actions of men of the physical environment, of the nervous system in general, and of the cerebral cortex in particular, of hormones, of conditioned reflexes, of social conditioning, of complexes, of passions and prejudices, of suggestion, of pseudo-logic, and of syntactically meaningless elaborations, even the judicious add their quota of erroneous logical explanations of non-logical actions. It is a useful exercise to read any general work of the first class of subjects while constantly bearing in mind the possibility of errors arising from the author's assumption that actions directly determined by the residues without the intervention of logic are on the contrary the result of logical analysis and that they may therefore admit of a logical interpretation which neglects the residues. I suggest the hypothesis that no one avoids such errors in writing (and *a fortiori* in talking) about the actions of men,[1] because I think some such mnemonic device a necessary condition for the advancement of science. The opposite error is probably rare, for intellectual tradition and habit both stand in its way.

The action of the residues as 'causes' is true to a first approximation. In a second approximation mutual dependence between residues and derivations is observed. Theological dogmas, laws, and even ethical derivations help to determine the formation of new residues. But in general neither sound reason nor derivations have much influence

---

[1] In order to avoid misunderstanding, I venture to point out that this hypothesis applies to the present essay. The reader should also note that the risk of falling into the opposite error is here exceptionally great. I have tried to be careful, but cannot be sure that I have succeeded in avoiding it.

upon the sentiments, which change slowly and, as it were, repel unwelcome intrusions. Thus it is easier to utilize the sentiments than to modify them. To know the residues and to utilize the sentiments that they represent has been a great part of the art of some of the greatest generals and rulers. With Caesar, Napoleon, Augustus, and Elizabeth such practices were plainly habitual. On the other hand, persistent effort to modify the sentiments of others has perhaps always been recognized by sensible men as a mark of immaturity, or of stupidity, or of lack of self-control. It is also well known as one of the pharmacological effects of alcohol.

The futility of a preoccupation with derivations and the absurdities that result from attempts to use systematic derivations as guides of conduct are often perceived by empiricists. They are probably still more often felt intuitively. This is perhaps the principal reason for the dislike of 'intellectuals' that is so commonly observed among skilful rulers, administrators, and men of affairs.

It follows from these considerations that the description of derivations and the analysis of their function in human societies are problems of great scientific importance. This is so because the derivations are commonly but erroneously treated as of the first importance in the determination of phenomena. Thus, there are many errors of ob-

servation and inference to be corrected and a new
departure to be taken. For this purpose the residues must supplant the derivations.

The discrimination and characterization of residues and derivations may be regarded as the foundation of Pareto's work. I believe that it is a firm
foundation, that it will serve for the study of any
of the interactions of men, and that it is indispensable, until improved upon, in the study of all
subjects of the first class.

Nothing is more striking in the history of science
than the immense services that have been rendered
at an early stage in the cultivation of every field by
simple discriminations, such as those of rational
and irrational numbers, mass and weight, force and
moment, mass and chemical equivalence, animals
that have red blood and other animals, the chemical and the thermodynamical aspects of metabo-
lism, infectious diseases and other diseases, and a
host of others. This first step, which is often difficult and which may cost much effort of the imag-
ination, lends meaning to observation, brings order
into memory, thereby greatly strengthening it, and
thus both directly and indirectly makes diagnosis
easy. In the advancement of science, the first step
is often not only the most costly but also the most
profitable and decisive. It is a remark of Mach's
that "the task of the early investigators who lay
the foundations is quite a different one from that

of their successors. The former have to seek out
and establish the weightiest facts only, and to do
this, as history teaches, calls for more intelligence
(Geist) than is generally believed." [1]

[1] Translated from E. Mach, *Die Mechanik in ihrer Entwickelung
historisch-kritisch Dargestellt*, 3rd edition, Leipzig, 1897, p. 73.

VI

CLASSIFICATION OF RESIDUES AND DERIVATIONS

THESE things, residues and derivations, must be classified to be known, and Pareto has classified them, the residues with mediocre success, the derivations very acceptably. The residues fall into six classes. He calls the first class the residues of combinations and the second, the persistent aggregates; these two classes serve his purpose well. Residues of the first class are attributes of inventors, speculators, politicians, and skilful leaders. Residues of the second class are found among those who are devoted to family, caste, church, and the community, in *rentiers*, and in good subordinates. A long list of them may be read in Montaigne's famous Essay, *Of Custom, and that an established law is not lightly to be changed*; [1] indeed many of the *Essays* of Montaigne are packed with illustrations of all sorts of residues, for Montaigne was one of the rare men who have half-intuitively perceived the importance of residues and the vanity of systematic derivations. This is probably one of the reasons

---

[1] *The Essays of Montaigne*, translated by E. J. Trechmann, London, 1927, Book I, Chap. 23, pp. 103–120.

why his writings are so unsystematic. For, in general, philosophical systems may be defined as systematic derivations from certain persistent aggregates (residues of the second class) of their authors, under the influence of the instinct of combinations (residues of the first class). Of this procedure Montaigne seems to have been both temperamentally (i.e. because he possessed a certain balance of residues) and intellectually (i.e. on logical grounds) incapable. This is well shown in his remark,[1] "We say, indeed, Power, Truth, Justice: they are words that denote something great, but that something we are quite unable to see and conceive." For this reason academic philosophers probably make no mistake in excluding the works of Montaigne from the history of philosophy.

At a later stage of his work Pareto devotes much time and effort to a study of the unequal distribution of residues of the first and second classes in different parts of a collectivity, of the utility of different proportions of these two classes of residues among rulers and ruled, and of the predominance of residues of the first class among 'speculators,' of residues of the second class among 'rentiers.' On the whole this extensive investigation, founded upon a wide knowledge of politics and of affairs, proves very fruitful of results. The remaining four

[1] *Op. cit.*, Book II, Chap. 12, p. 494.

classes of residues provide useful labels for the facts
and hardly serve any other purpose.

The six classes of residues are as follows:

I. Instinct of combinations.

II. Persistence of aggregates.

III. The need of manifesting sentiments by
external acts.

IV. Residues relating to sociability.

V. The integrity of the individual and of
what he considers dependent upon him.

VI. The sexual residue.

Pareto was aware of the inadequacy of this classification. But there is much to be said for it. I venture to suggest that long experience in the natural
sciences has taught the inestimable advantage of
any classification over none, and I think that
Pareto knew what he was about when he made
shift with a classification that did not please him,
as an aid in a wide survey of facts.[1]

The classification and description of derivations
is perhaps the most finished portion of the whole
work. At this point some of the leading ideas may
have arisen from Bacon's *Idols* or from other
sources, but the hard substance of this remarkable
study is Pareto's. Like Bacon, he too was a man of
the world and a scholar. If he was not a lord chan-
cellor, he had other advantages as an engineer and
scientist, and behind him were three hundred years

[1] See note 10 below, p. 105.

more of experience. In his study of the derivations he knew how to exploit all his advantages.

Pareto distinguished four classes of derivations:

    I. Affirmation.

    II. Authority.

    III. Accord with sentiments or with principles.

    IV. Verbal proofs.

An example of the first class is the taboo without sanction. Another common example is the unfounded assertion introduced in the course of an argument, which benefits from the assent given to the propositions that it accompanies.

Examples of the second class are familiar to all. If we may judge from the current practices of many American advertisers, the expression of an opinion by any person whose name is known to the public, on any subject, regardless of the person's competency to form an opinion on the subject, will influence the actions of many readers of the opinion. Since the decisive factor in determining the policy of advertising is variation of sales, the evidence seems fairly conclusive.

There are endless examples of higher authorities, like those of Homer for the Greeks, and of the Bible for Christians. As Pareto notes, it would be difficult to say what has not been found in the Bible. And there are the many cases of the authority of traditions, such as the traditions of American college students. Appeal to the authority of custom is also common, as in the phrases "play the game" and "that isn't done." It remains to note the obvious case of the authority of a divinity or of a personification.

The existence of certain types of derivations of the third class has been widely recognized, for example, by Caesar in the remark,[1] "homines id quod volunt credunt," and by Bacon, who says,[2] "The human understanding is no dry light but receives an infusion from the will and affections; whence proceed sciences which may be called 'sciences as one would.' For what a man had rather were true he more readily believes. Therefore he rejects difficult things from impatience of research; sober things, because they narrow hope; the deeper things of nature, from superstition; the light of experience, from arrogance and pride, lest his mind should seem to be occupied with things mean and transitory; things not commonly believed, out of deference to the opinion of the vulgar. Numberless in short are the ways, and sometimes imperceptible, in which the affections color and infect the understanding."

Bacon's reference to the unconscious character of wishful thinking is especially notable. Indeed, this whole aphorism is a good description of the kind of

[1] De Bello Gallico, Book III, Chap. 18.
[2] Novum Organum, Book I, Aphorism XLIX.

derivations now extensively studied by psychoanalysts under the name of rationalizations. The
expression *dry light* is derived from Heraclitus,[1] and
if Bacon's interpretation of the passage is correct,
Heraclitus's phrase may be the earliest explicit
reference to wishful thinking that is now known.

Pareto's analysis of this class of derivations is
far more detailed, systematic, and extensive than
earlier discussions of the subject. It does not admit
of summary treatment, but must be studied in the
original.

The fourth class of derivations, verbal proofs,
occupy the whole of Chapter X of the Treatise.
The exposition of them is even less amenable than
that of the third class to brief description, but, I
think, it is an equally profitable subject matter of
study. The derivations of the fourth class include
Bacon's *Idols of the Market Place.*

The reader will find in Chapter X, carefully ar-
ranged and clearly presented, verbal derivations of
many of the most famous authors of works on history, philosophy, sociology, and religion. It must
be an exceptional person indeed who can read this
chapter understandingly without discovering the
nature and the source of many of his own errors.

Throughout the Treatise Pareto takes pains to
avoid in his own discussions the ambiguities and

[1] Cf. Diels, *Die Fragmente der Vorsokratiker*, Berlin, 1903, p. 82,
§ 118.

other difficulties that result from the use of words, to explain them and to warn against them, and one of his most important and constantly repeated precepts is: *Never dispute about words.* To these ends he makes frequent use of letters instead of words as symbols for carefully formulated definitions, and he also employs letters as a test for verbal derivations. Since this test is often surprisingly useful and effective, it may be illustrated by an example. Jeans says:[1] "If the universe is a universe of thought, then its creation must have been an act of thought." This is an enthymeme, and therefore suspect. Substituting X for *thought*, we have: If the universe is a universe of X, then its creation must have been an act of X. This should suffice to reveal the derivation, but if it does not, some other word like *love* or *matter* may now be substituted for X. A similar result may be obtained by putting Y in place of *creation* and then, if necessary, replacing Y by another word like *evolution*.

Bacon says,[2] "The doctrine of idols is to the interpretation of nature what the doctrine of the refutation of sophisms is to common logic." A moment's reflection will show that here Bacon is both discriminating between two different classes of phenomena and also asserting the need of recognizing the nature of derivations and the small im-

---

[1] J. H. Jeans, *The Mysterious Universe*, New York, 1930, p. 154.
[2] Novum Organum, Book I, Aphorism XL.

portance of understanding the fallacies of logic in the business of science and of everyday life.

Bacon's assertion depends upon the theorem, not stated by Pareto but fully established by an induction from his study of derivations, that nearly all speech, whether in the form of conversation or of oratory or of debate, and nearly all writing, except the most careful scientific writing and colorless statements of concrete sensory experience, are full of derivations. This theorem holds for all men, always, everywhere. It is a useful one for those who can apply it to their own behavior, as well as to the behavior of others. But to do so is difficult, for pleasure in one's own derivations is no small part of the pleasure of speaking and writing, and the sentiments form a barrier to the opportune recollection and use of the theorem. In this connection, I may point out that the reader should not permit his approval or disapproval of my statement, "this theorem holds for all men, always, everywhere," to lead him to forget the implicit qualifications: approximately, probably.

The theorem is also useful as a means of demonstrating the function of derivations when they are in the place to which they are adapted and thus refuting the opinion that they are intrinsically 'harmful,' 'objectionable,' or 'valueless.' For it is now clear that the beauty of literature may be often ascribed in a first approximation to form and the effective use of derivations. Extreme instances are Ariel's songs in *The Tempest* and *The Ancient Mariner*. In short, derivations, like residues, are intrinsically neither 'good' nor 'bad.' They are useful, or negligible, or harmful in respect of, or relatively to, their place or function.

As our quotations from Bacon show, many of the facts of derivation have long been known and recorded. But they have been hardly ever weighed and little used in the social sciences, where it is perhaps most necessary to take account of them. In order that they may be used, an effective mnemonic device is required. I suggest that Pareto's analysis of the derivations yields the best one I know, and present the theorem stated above as a convenient formulation of the most general result of that analysis.

Making derivations and mistaking mutual dependence for cause and effect are the two important modes (i.e. the two known important modes) of false reasoning.[1] They may appear separately, but are not independent, because the desire for simple explanations is a powerful sentiment which sometimes becomes irresistible. Thus the devil is needed to explain evil, and particular devils are

[1] Recent developments in logic suggest that for some future purposes it may be convenient to distinguish psychological, semantical, and syntactical elements in derivations, or at least in derivations of the fourth class. Perhaps therefore the reference to the making of derivations as a single mode of false reasoning is over-simple.

gratifying when particular evils afflict us. A case in point is the belief of many Germans that the diabolical Sir Edward Grey caused the World War. This belief persisted for months and years in the face of the evidence that Grey's influence, in so far as it tended toward war, was probably the result of his integrity and devotion to principles that inopportunely limited his freedom of action,[1] and thus prevented decisions based upon the consideration of expediency (logical actions) and led to decisions based upon his sense of honor (non-logical actions). Similar examples from all the other nations could be given. Finally we may note that, like the devil himself, the more abstract explanations of this kind often become residues in the form of persistent aggregates such as capitalism for socialists, communism for the rich, and microbes for hypochondriacs.

[1] See Reinach's definition of religion, below, p. 52.

VII

SYNTHESIS

THE last half of the book is synthetic, but like all the rest it is enriched with a profusion of diverse and well chosen facts. Pareto works up to his social system, then defines it, and finally tests it in a survey of important aspects of the history of Europe. We can no longer follow him here with a summary, for these eight hundred pages are incompressible.[1] To some readers they will seem to be prolegomena to a philosophy of history. But this view would be misleading, for they are chiefly the result of Pareto's singularly pertinacious effort to make use of his instrument and method in the study of the actual social systems that were known to him. So far as he was able, he approached this task in the spirit of a scientific investigator.

Long before, he had written:[2] "Each of us has within a secret adversary who tries to prevent him . . . from abstaining from the mixture of his own sentiments with logical deductions from facts. In

---

[1] For a valuable methodical analysis of the Treatise, the reader may consult *An Introduction to Pareto, His Sociology*, by G. C. Homans and C. P. Curtis, Jr., New York, 1934.

[2] Pareto, *Les Systèmes Socialistes*, Vol. I, p. 6, 2nd edition, par les soins de G. H. Bousquet, Paris, 1926.

noting this general defect, I well know that I am
not exempt. My sentiments lead me to favor freedom; therefore I have taken pains to react against
them. But it may be that I have gone too far and,
fearing to give too much weight to the arguments in
favor of freedom, have not given them enough
weight. Similarly, it is possible that, fearing to give
too little weight to sentiments that I do not share,
I have given them too much. In any case, since I
am not quite sure that this source of error is absent, it is my duty to point it out."

Such was Pareto's position when he began his
sociological studies. It never changed. But, as we
have seen, one of the most valuable results of these
studies was the demonstration of the well-nigh
universal presence, except in the most austere
sciences, of derivations in the writings of men; we
may again recall, noting the change of reference
from the original, *quod ab omnibus, quod ubique,
quod semper*. Thus from long frequentation and
familiarity Pareto became even more amply aware
of the danger, and, like an experienced physician,
almost intuitively aware of it. Nevertheless, in the
course of his labors he frequently lightened his
effort and permitted himself the relief of paren-
thetical expressions of certain sentiments. But
these interjections, written while clearly aware of
what he is doing, are no more than asides that leave
the substance of the work unchanged. On the other

hand, it is probable that he had not acquired complete immunity to the dangerous practice of deriving, and that from time to time he unconsciously fell into errors of the kind that he so well describes. Indeed he has, I think, demonstrated that complete immunity to thinking in derivations is impossible. We may note Pareto's dislike of sentimentality as a probable source of errors of this kind. I also suspect that in the face of loss of self-control by others he did not always remain imperturbable, and sometimes unconsciously reacted to derivations with derivations of his own. The physiological basis of this form of behavior is so firm, its biophysical and biochemical components are often so far beyond even indirect voluntary control, that escape is perhaps not always possible for even the most self-controlled thinkers. On the other hand, I believe that he did sometimes 'lean over backwards,' as he suggests in the above quotation, when seeking to avoid the influence of his own residues. Only experience and further cultivation of the field can discover and correct the errors that may have been introduced in such ways. Having set down these sources of unconscious derivations that I have come to suspect in Pareto's work, it is well that I should add that I do not suspect any others, apart from quite exceptional and negligible accidents, and that I should warn the reader that I feel far from sure that even such errors have produced any measurable modifications of Pareto's more general results, and that I have slowly reached the conclusion, after long and careful study, that, among all the works of the first class, broad in scope, with which I am familiar, such defects are least frequent in Pareto's Treatise.

I hope that it will now be clear that the prevalent description of Pareto as the Karl Marx of the bourgeoisie or of fascism is nothing more than a derivation. It is a fact that Signor Mussolini has attributed his abandonment of socialism to the teaching of Pareto, and it is said that in Italy and in Germany Pareto's work is much esteemed, though perhaps it is not always understood by the more enthusiastic. But his writings are no less applicable to France, England, the United States, and Russia than to Italy and Germany, and Pareto himself preferred to all other governments those of some of the smaller Swiss cantons.[1]

Throughout this last section of the Treatise, Pareto is concerned with residues, derivations, heterogeneity, and the economic interests in their state of mutual dependence. But in the main the residues of the first and second classes do the work of all the residues and the 'circulation of the elite' is the only aspect of social heterogeneity that is

[1] Treatise, § 2240, note 1: an exceptional instance in this work of the expression of a concrete judgment of utility, unsupported by evidence and analysis.

given a careful systematic analysis. Certain special features of this part of the book may now be considered.

The treatment of equilibrium, which is referred to in note 4, is logically of great significance. Pareto observes that the state of the social system is determined by its conditions. Therefore, if a small modification of the state of the system is imposed upon it, a reaction will take place and this will tend to restore the original state, very slightly modified by the experience.[1] This principle is well known, and the corresponding facts are familiar to everybody. Thus the disturbances produced by short wars, by epidemics that are not too severe, and by all kinds of lesser catastrophies ordinarily disappear and leave hardly a trace behind them. The case of physiological equilibrium is similar. In fact it is logically identical. When recovery from disease is in question the process is still often referred to as a result of the *vis medicatrix naturae*. Claude Bernard's discussion of the constancy of the *milieu intérieur* [2] bears on the same point, and so do Cannon's recent discussion of homeostasis [3] and Barcroft's still more recent book.[4]

---

[1] See note 11 below, p. 110.

[2] C. Bernard, *An Introduction to the Study of Experimental Medicine*, New York, 1927, p. 98.

[3] W. B. Cannon, *The Wisdom of the Body*, New York, 1932.

[4] J. Barcroft, *The Architecture of Physiological Function*, Cambridge, England, 1934.

It is instructive to note that these physiological phenomena have been used by philosophers as a foundation of the argument for vitalism. For they belong in the same class as those inorganic processes that arise from similar disturbances of physical and chemical equilibrium. This is implied by the similarity of Pareto's definition of equilibrium — a state such that if a small modification different from that which will otherwise occur is imposed upon a system, a reaction will at once appear, tending toward the conditions that would have existed if the modification had not been imposed — with the theorem of Le Chatelier in thermodynamics. The wide bearing of this theorem was long ago pointed out by Bancroft.[1]

Since the general characteristics of such phenomena as those designated by Pareto's definition of equilibrium are well known from wide experience, and since the facts show that the phenomena exist in social systems, Pareto is able to make use of this wide experience in his study of the social system. This he does to good purpose, in spite of the lack of quantitative data.

The treatment of utility is another striking feature of the book. Noting first that the choice of a norm or judge of utility is arbitrary, Pareto falls back on the known properties of equilibrium and

[1] W. D. Bancroft, Journal of the American Chemical Society, Vol. XXXIII, 1911, p. 92.

remarks that whatever choice may be made of a norm or a judge, the entities that are determined by the choice will possess certain properties. In particular, increasing utility will involve approach to a limiting condition which is determined by the choice of the norm. But utility defined by such an arbitrary choice must be distinguished from the utility of ordinary language, with which it may coincide in some cases, but from which in other cases it may differ completely. Thus, choosing material prosperity as a norm will give one result; choosing the ideal of the ascetics, another.

Pareto next proceeds to a scrupulous explanation of the difficulties that such ambiguities produce and then distinguishes the following special utilities:

(a) Utility of an individual:
   1. Direct utility.
   2. Indirect utility, obtained because the individual is a part of a collectivity.
   3. Utility of an individual, in relation with the utilities of other individuals.
(b) Utility of a collectivity, with distinctions similar to those that precede:
   1. Direct utility, considered separately from other collectivities.
   2. Indirect utility, obtained by the influence of other collectivities.
   3. Utility of a collectivity, in relation with the utilities of other collectivities.

Far from agreeing, these utilities are often plainly in opposition. Moreover, the question of present and future utilities presents further familiar complications; for example, in deciding whether to spend or to save.

The question of total utility now arises as a still further complication and this is followed by a long and difficult discussion of maximum utility, based upon known properties of the economic system and upon a further distinction between utility *of* a collectivity and utility *for* a collectivity. This distinction arises from the fact that a collectivity can be considered as a unity and also as a collection of individuals, and that it is convenient to consider it in both aspects.

The discussion, which cannot be summarized, reveals explicitly and in detail and, I think, makes quite clear the logical complications of this problem. After reading and understanding it, no one can fail to see that expressions like *the greatest happiness of the greatest number* are meaningless derivations.[1] I hope that it will now be evident, however, that they are not for this reason unimportant or lacking in social utility. But this importance

[1] More than a half century ago Edgeworth wrote: "That the great Bentham should have adopted as the creed of his life and watchword of his party an expression which is meant to be quantitatively precise, and yet when scientifically analysed may appear almost unmeaning, is significant of the importance to be attached to the science of quantity [and of derivations]. 'Greatest happiness of the greatest number' — is this more intelligible than 'greatest illumination with the greatest number of lamps'?" F. Y. Edgeworth, *Mathematical Psychics*, London, 1881, p. 117.

and this utility should be ascribed mainly to the corresponding residues.

The distinction between the utility of a collectivity and utility for a collectivity may be illustrated by considering the increase of the population of a country. The utility of the collectivity can, in general, be increased, as a result of increased military and political power, by an increase of population up to the point where national impoverishment first sets in. Certain hostile critics believe that the recent policy of Italy has been based upon this consideration. But the point at which increase of population leads to maximum utility for the collectivity, that is to say, to a distribution of individual utilities that seems to yield a maximum, appears to be lower. The reader should remember, however, that the positions of these maxima depend upon the choice of norms, that different judges and critics will choose different norms, that each choice is arbitrary, and that there is no known logical operation which yields a choice between these arbitrary choices.

Another example of the consideration of the utility of a collectivity may be cited, because of present interest in the question. Pareto analyzes the relation of the European socialist parties of a quarter century ago to the utility of the collectivity in which they existed. He reaches the conclusion that the discipline of their position as members of a party had greatly increased the self-respect and self-control (residues of the fifth class: integrity of the individual) of many of the working class members of the parties, and he believes that this may be very favorable to the welfare of (i.e. may have 'survival value' for) a collectivity. On the other hand, he has formed a low estimate of the influence of membership in the socialist parties and of the corresponding activities on their middle class members. This difference he ascribes to the different residues that are concerned in the two cases.

Pareto's analysis of ideal ends is another good example of the use of his conceptual scheme in disentangling the complex elements of a general problem.

The abstract definition of the social system and of the properties of equilibrium are also employed by Pareto in a study of some of the great undulatory movements of history. This ambitious undertaking necessarily remains fragmentary, and I shall not try to describe it.

Religion is a subject to which Pareto devotes much attention, and since he reaches certain definite conclusions that bear upon the functions of religion and of morals in concrete social systems, it may be appropriate to bring our examples to an end with this topic.

The first serious approach to the subject in the Treatise is an examination of the differences of

opinion between Salomon Reinach [1] and Father
M. J. Lagrange [2] concerning the definition of the
word religion. Reinach, whose position is probably
unfriendly to existing religions, states his definition
in his work, *Orpheus, A General History of Religions*.
In a characteristic aside of the kind that I have
above described, Pareto remarks that perhaps this
work would be better named, *A General History of
Religions Seen in the Light of the Dreyfus Case*.
Reinach defines religion as "a system of scruples
that present an obstacle to the free exercise of our
faculties."

Father Lagrange objects to this definition. As
Pareto points out, Lagrange can accept it only
"under penalty of suicide," and he, in turn, defines religion, but quite differently, as "the belief
in superior powers with which one can establish
relations."

Having noted the positions adopted by the two
parties to the controversy, Pareto proceeds to a
meticulous and exceedingly systematic analysis.
This involves careful preliminary logical considerations; next, the designation of Reinach's religion as
religion *a* and of Lagrange's as religion *β*, and then
a methodical demonstration that both religion *a*
and religion *β* are present in many phenomena that

[1] *Orpheus*, New York, 1930, p. 3.
[2] *Quelques remarques sur l'Orpheus de M. Salomon Reinach*, Paris,
1910.

are commonly called religions. However, religion
a is a more common phenomenon than religion β,
for religion a is found without religion β in taboos
and fetiches, in the religion of Comte, etc. But, on
the other hand, religion β is sometimes found un-
accompanied by religion a. Finally, there is at least
one case where the first part of religion β is not
accompanied by the second part. Pareto notes
that these facts show very clearly how unsuitable
the terms of ordinary language are for the purposes
of scientific classification and then closes the discussion with an important observation. The two
definitions are of diverse natures; they lead to the
discrimination of different kinds of facts, Reinach's definition to residues and Lagrange's to
derivations.

Pareto agrees with the opinion of Machiavelli
quoted at the beginning of this Essay, concerning
the utility of the early Roman religion, but he car-
ries the analysis farther, showing that this religion
was primarily concerned with cult and not in any
substantial measure with interpretation or imag-
ination. This cult, which was in a state of mutual
dependence with the residues (including the manifestations of Reinach's scruples) indirectly modified, by way of the sentiments, the actions of the
early Romans, thus helping to produce "well regulated conduct," just as Machiavelli explains.

Pareto also examines the problem of the utility

interests of society. When an individual in the society possesses useful sentiments, it is of little or no importance with what derivations from them he satisfies his need of explanations.

An example of the role of the persistent aggregates of religion may make all this clearer. The formalism of the Roman religion was in a state of mutual dependence with the formalism of everyday life, of law, and of politics. Each strengthened and was strengthened by the others. Thus up to the period of the end of the republic this formalism permitted much liberty without danger of anarchy. But finally the old Roman persistent aggregates were in great measure dislocated by political, social, and economic changes, and replaced by the residues of newcomers of other nationalities. With this modification of the residues the old freedom had become impossible, and despotism was thenceforth unavoidable. It may be noted that new residues were slowly adapted to this necessity.

These few illustrations of the contents of the last part of the Treatise might be multiplied many times, but for further information it will be more profitable to consult the original in its full extent.

VIII

CONCLUSION

On some persons this book has an effect like that
frequently produced by the works of Machiavelli.
For similar reasons, similar sentiments are stirred.
Among these reasons the chief is that both Machiavelli and Pareto "write what men do and not what
they ought to do." In order to understand this it is
necessary to distinguish between subjects, like the
science of government as conceived by Machiavelli, that chiefly include the residues and derivations of others, and writings, like Plato's *Republic*,
that chiefly exhibit the author's own residues and
derivations.

It is often said that Pareto's position is anti-
intellectual. If the term anti-intellectual is defined so as to make the statement true, it is true.
He held that a scientist's own residues and derivations are out of place in science. He demonstrated
the abundant presence of certain kinds of residues
and derivations in the writings of social scientists
and explained how this condition interferes with
the advancement of learning. He also held that
the influence of these particular residues and derivations in the determination of public policy is

disastrous. He says,[1] "Like Chinese mandarins,
European 'intellectuals' are the worst of rulers;
and the fact that European 'intellectuals' have
played a less important role than mandarins in
government is one of the numerous reasons why the
fate of the peoples of Europe has been different
from that of the Chinese." [2] Does this perchance
classify the failure of Woodrow Wilson and his intelligent advisors or of Mr. Hoover's commissions
and surveys, on the one hand, and the success of
the nineteenth century English policy of muddling
through, on the other?

Pareto's whole life was devoted mainly to science, and few have surveyed science more broadly,
or more shrewdly analyzed it. His sociology is
the culminating work of this long life, a synthesis
of his wide experience. Industry, skill, method,
encyclopedic knowledge, initiative, originality,
stubborn consecutive continuous thought are
terms that describe it. It is a scientific treatise.

This book bears all the marks of the spade-work
of a pioneer. Therefore, no sensible and experienced man will suppose that it is free from numerous and important errors of fact, or from mistakes
of inference and judgment. Above all, it is incon-
ceivable that the treatment of such a subject should
be complete and exhaustive. But Pareto's errors

[1] Treatise § 2229.
[2] See note 12 below, p. 115.

and omissions will come to light if the work is continued, and this work is of the kind, being scientific, that can be continued *by others*. Thus, sooner or later, it will be superseded in use by that which will rest upon it as a foundation. No one knew this better than Pareto, who took pleasure in saying that the sooner his sociology was supplanted, the greater its success would be. Meanwhile, it is an indispensable book.

Postscript

Having now to the best of my ability defined the relevant terms and described the nature of the phenomena that are involved, I may, perhaps, without undue risk of misunderstanding,[1] give myself the pleasure of making a derivation of the first class my last word to the reader: Pareto's Treatise is a work of genius.

[1] See note 13 below, p. 118.

NOTES

NOTES

NOTE 1

SENTIMENTS: DEFINITION OF THE TERM AND DISCUSSION OF MACHIAVELLI'S SENTIMENTS

Throughout this essay the word *sentiment* [1] is used in a very general sense, and in conformity with Pareto's use as I interpret it. It implies nothing concerning psychological processes. It refers to no psychological theories or classifications. These things are not here in question. It does refer to a hypothetical psychical state, or to some part or aspect of such a hypothetical state. Examples of sentiments, as the term is here used, are the hypothetical entities vaguely referred to by the following words and phrases: A desire to solve a scientific problem, a feeling that justice exists, a sense of the value of certain customs and rites, a need to participate in the acts of a cult, a feeling of personal integrity, a sense of loyalty to a community, a sexual complex. Sentiments are not here regarded as facts. The actions and expressions of men are facts. In some instances these actions and expressions are regarded, for convenience, as manifestations of sentiments. Sentiments are not regarded as either real or unreal. In this respect they are regarded as forces are regarded in modern dynamics. Therefore, the existence of an assumed sentiment is neither proved nor disproved by ex-

[1] See above, p. 5.

perience; but with the aid of the assumption (as with the aid of the assumption of a force in mechanics), a uniformity in the facts is discovered, and in this case the assumption is retained for further use; or a uniformity is not discovered, and in this case the assumption is abandoned.

Having made this meaning clear, once for all, I shall continue to use the common forms of expression, and beg the reader to apply the above stated qualifications. If he finds the use of the word sentiment, for any reason, inconvenient when this meaning is assigned to it, I urge him to choose any other word whatever as the bearer of this meaning and to employ it wherever I have used the word sentiment. In this connection it may be convenient to note that the purpose of this definition of the word sentiment is so far as possible, within limits that seem unavoidable, to separate and distinguish direct observation, on the one hand, and interpretation, on the other hand.

In Machiavelli's writings it is occasionally possible to find the expressions of two sentiments: (1) the desire to promote his private interests and (2) Italian patriotism. But such expressions are rare, and significantly absent, or nearly so, from the body of his works. For the first, the dedication of *The Prince* may be consulted; for the second, the final chapter of the same work. But neither of these sentiments can have had much to do in determining the reputation of Machiavelli's works, and, so far as may be seen, neither seems to have greatly modified the scientific results. Therefore, we are on neither count here concerned with them.

Perhaps the chief source of the evil reputation of
Machiavelli is an important characteristic of his
writings that is widely, and possibly incorrectly,
regarded as the manifestation of the author's un-
scrupulous and malevolent nature. This troublesome subject may be analyzed and made clear by
taking an example. In the eighteenth chapter of
The Prince, Machiavelli says, ". . . he who has
known best how to employ the fox has succeeded
best. But it is necessary to know well how to dis-
guise this characteristic, and to be a great pre-
tender and dissembler; and men are so simple, and
so subject to present necessities, that he who seeks
to deceive will always find some one who will allow
himself to be deceived." This statement goes beyond an induction, or statement of observed uniformities, in that Machiavelli makes an assertion of
the form: In order that A shall occur, B is necessary. This form of statement is no less familiar in
scientific writing, is, in short, no less 'scientific'
than the statement of an induction. For instance
one may say: In order that an eclipse shall occur,
it is necessary that the three bodies, sun, earth, and
moon, shall move simultaneously into positions
that fall in one straight line. Applied science is
made up in great part of such theorems. When
such assertions are made in ordinary language, the
use of words like *necessary* and *must* is practically
unavoidable, and when voluntary human actions
are in question, the use of the word *ought* is hardly
less so; thus we say, if a man would accomplish A, he
ought to do B. In like manner Machiavelli says in
Chapter XVII of *The Prince*, "Therefore a prince,

so long as he keeps his subjects united and loyal, ought not to mind the reproach of cruelty." *The Prince* is full of such statements, which, apart from a distaste for the subject as a whole, are probably the chief source of Machiavelli's evil reputation.

Such theorems are the results, correct or incorrect as the case may be, of Machiavelli's careful analysis of the facts. They may merely involve the use of words resembling *should* or *ought* in the sense just noted. Thus, the assertion, "in order to accomplish A a man ought to do B," means *at least* that B is one of the necessary conditions for the existence of A, without any implications concerning right and wrong, or justice, or duty, and it *may be* intended to mean no more.

If we were here concerned with the scientific study of Machiavelli's special problems, it would be necessary to find out how far the facts appear to bear out Machiavelli's conclusions, when they are interpreted in this manner. Even then it would hardly serve any useful purpose to know how far, or to what end, Machiavelli intended to give advice and counsel, how far, in short, his use of words like *should* and *ought* implies something more than the inference from observed uniformities that certain results will probably follow from certain actions. But it will be useful to note that dislike of Machiavelli's conclusions has probably led many readers to attribute to him a much stronger desire to give evil counsel than is warranted by a careful, dispassionate examination and analysis of his writings.

In brief, the chief scientific characteristics of

Machiavelli's political works seem to be (1) a study of the interrelations of the sentiments, the interests, and the actions of men, (2) the formulation of inductions from the facts, and (3) the deduction of theorems (a) that from certain actions certain results will probably follow, and (b) that to attain certain ends, certain actions will probably be effective. These characteristics are so evident and Machiavelli's success is so great, that there can be little doubt about the sentiments and motives that dominated the man, at least while he was doing his work. It is a well founded psychological induction that such work is always done whole-heartedly. But there is also evidence in this case. Writing to Francesco Vettori on 13 December, 1513, Machiavelli said: [1] "The evening being come, I return home and go to my study; at the entrance I pull off my peasant-clothes, covered with dust and dirt, and put on my noble court dress, and thus becomingly re-clothed I pass into the ancient courts of the men of old, where, being lovingly received by them, I am fed with that food which is mine alone; where I do not hesitate to speak with them, and to ask for the reason of their actions, and they in their benignity answer me; and for four hours I feel no weariness, I forget every trouble, poverty does not dismay, death does not terrify me; I am possessed entirely by those great men. And because Dante says:

Knowledge doth come of learning well retained,
Unfruitful else,

[1] Quoted from *The Prince*, by Niccolo Machiavelli, translated by W. K. Marriott (Everyman's Library), pp. xv, xvi. My quotations from *The Prince* are also taken from Marriott's edition.

I have noted down what I have gained from their conversation, and have composed a small work on 'Principalities,' where I pour myself out as fully as I can in meditation on the subject, discussing what a principality is, what kinds there are, how they can be acquired, how they can be kept, why they are lost. . . ." Such was Machiavelli's experience in doing his work, and, in spite of differences in the external conditions, Pareto's experience in writing his Treatise was similar, and so perhaps is that of all first-rate craftsmen when they are making their masterpieces. One looks in vain for the manifestation of other sentiments in the prosecution of such work.

It is perhaps impossible to make a dispassionate estimate of Machiavelli's desire that his conclusions and theorems should find practical applications. In certain instances this desire seems to be pretty clearly manifested in his works, but in general it is not. Moreover, it seems very probable that Machiavelli was aware of the distinction between a necessary condition and a necessary *and* sufficient condition, as well as of the great importance of this distinction in making plans by means of deductions from general principles. In short, I think he probably knew that his results were inadequate to the needs of the practical politician. Nothing that we know of his character seems inconsistent with a desire that his theorems should find practical applications, which may have been strengthened by his private interests and by his patriotism. On the other hand, we have just noted that his language, especially in *The Prince*, can hardly fail to lead all readers, or at least those whose sentiments are hostile, to an exaggerated estimate of the strength of this desire. This question is no more important from a scientific standpoint for sociology than the question of the motives of Euclid or of Newton is for mathematics or physics.

NOTE 2

DURKHEIM'S STUDY OF THE SENTIMENTS

This statement [1] will hardly find favor with some readers. It may, therefore, be useful by way of illustration to consider certain aspects of the works of Durkheim, an eminent sociologist who devoted much time and effort to the study of the influence of the sentiments upon human affairs. His failures in scientific description and logical analysis, in spite of notable success in other aspects of his work, are, I believe, not unlike the failures of many others, and, in any case, the present discussion had better be founded upon concrete facts. The facts that I shall consider are statements of Durkheim's. I shall consider them because I think that it will occur to many that he was a predecessor of Pareto in the scientific description and logical analysis of the influence of the sentiments upon human affairs. So, in a measure, he was, but his attempt to prove the existence of a metaphysical entity singularly modified his work. Two examples will make my meaning clear.

Durkheim says,[2] ". . . we have here a class of

[1] See above, p. 7.

[2] E. Durkheim, translated from *Les Règles de la Méthode Sociologique*, 7th edition, Paris, 1919, p. 8.

facts that present the following very special characteristics: They consist of manners of acting,
thinking, and feeling, exterior to the individual, that
possess a power of coercion by virtue of which they
impose themselves upon him."

Again in discussing the customary explanations
of domestic organization as dependent upon the
sentiments of parents for children, of economic
activity as dependent upon the desire for wealth,
etc., Durkheim, who objects to such explanations,
says: [1] "But such a method is not applicable to
sociological phenomena without denaturing them.
To have the proof of this assertion it is sufficient to
note the definition that we have given of sociological phenomena. Since their essential characteristic consists in the power that they possess of
exerting from the outside a pressure on individual
consciousness, it must be that they do not derive
from individual consciousness and, accordingly,
that sociology is not a corollary of psychology."

To me the first of these quotations is a meaningless statement, for I conceive thinking and feeling
as activities of, or associated with, nervous systems which are parts of individuals. I prefer the
following very different statement: The actions,
thoughts, and feelings of individuals depend upon
the present condition, the past condition, the rate
of change, etc., of society and of its parts. They
also depend upon other factors, e.g. age, sex, concentration of alcohol in the blood, body temperature, external temperature, weather, mental com-

[1] *Op. cit.*, p. 124.

plexes, and, notably, conditioning that has been received in early years, etc.

What Durkheim has in mind seem to be, at least in part, the phenomena now rather vaguely designated by the term conditioning. On this subject the physiological researches of Pavlov concerning conditioned reflexes have yielded much information. Meanwhile, the studies of Malinowski and others have greatly advanced our knowledge of the allied sociological phenomena among primitive peoples. The upshot of all this recent work justifies Durkheim's insistence upon the facts and proves him to have been a skilful diagnostician. But "manners of acting, thinking, and feeling, exterior to the individual" have been forgotten or remain unknown to such investigators. The phenomena here in question are included in Pareto's residues of the second, third, and fourth classes.

The second quotation also presents other difficulties, and several remarks are to the point. (1) Durkheim, thinking of action, forgets reaction, in spite of the fact that this appears in Newton's third law and that it has been observed in all kinds of phenomena, including countless sociological phenomena; for instance, in the operation of sumptuary and prohibitory laws. (2) Taking account of a neglected factor does not 'denature phenomena.' It is the practice of all sciences to do this. For example, in the study of gases, after a relation between pressure and volume had been discovered, a relation between pressure, volume, and temperature was found and then quantities were introduced into the mathematical expression to allow

for what were believed to be the space occupied by
the molecules of the gas and the action of these
molecules upon one another. So also, in the study
of the recent history of Germany, the facts may be
first interpreted 'materialistically.' Later, the influence of the peculiarities of the Junker class may
be added to the analysis, next the results of the
traditions of the army, and then the results of the
thoughts and sentiments of Bismarck and William
the First, of Bülow and William the Second, etc.
In fact, this kind of analysis has always been found
necessary as a means of synthesis. (3) The difficulty seems to be due to Durkheim's conception of
cause and effect. Very generally in sociology, as
in physiology, all (i.e. every persistent factor) is
cause and all is effect. But Durkheim discovers
statistical correlations and thinks that they must
have a unique explanation, which by a perversion
of the logic of statistics and probability [1] he then
discovers. He believes that things proceed from
cause to effect, according to a naive and inadmis-
sible view of causation. But it is obvious that when
Durkheim says "since their essential characteristic
consists in the power which they possess of exerting from the outside a pressure on individual consciousness, it must be that they do not derive from
individual consciousness" he is asserting for a special case that since y is a function of x, x cannot be a
function of y. This is absurd, and, I venture to
think, an example of one of the most dangerous fallacies that a sociologist can fall into. It is a well

[1] E. Durkheim, *Le Suicide*, Paris, 1930, Livre III, Chap. I, especially p. 348.

established fact that Durkheim's concrete sociological entities (of course I am not speaking of his
metaphysical embodiment of them) not only act
upon but are acted upon by individual consciousness. Indeed I have little doubt that what Durkheim meant to say was different from what he said;
for it is certain that while expressing his conclusions metaphysically, he was, on the whole, guided
by the facts in the further prosecution of his researches. But such descriptions as those here in
question are not scientific descriptions, and such
analyses are not logical analyses.

The belief that sciences must be kept in water-
tight compartments is widely held by philosophers,
but no longer by scientists. I know of only two
justifications for anything like this opinion: (1) It is
a good plan to know what you are doing. This is
ground, as a convenience, for a temporary water-
tight compartment and seems to be one reason for
the importance of Durkheim's study of facts. (2)
In the formulation of a fairly complete science it is
excellent to be methodical.

To Durkheim's procedure one may apply Bacon's remark: [1] "For he had come to his conclusion before; he did not consult experience, as he
should have done, in order to the framing of his
decisions and axioms; but having first determined
the question according to his will, he then resorts
to experience, and bending her into conformity
with his placets leads her about like a captive in a
procession."

[1] Novum Organum, Book I, Aphorism LXIII.

I present the above criticism of Durkheim's opinions and practices as an example, thinking that similar criticisms apply to the works of many others, and hoping thus to illustrate the meaning of my assertion that from Machiavelli to Pareto there had been very little advance in *scientific description* and *logical analysis* of the influence of the sentiments upon human affairs.

NOTE 3

QUANTITATIVE DESCRIPTION OF A PHYSICO-CHEMICAL SYSTEM

Even an excessively simple example of the method that enables us to escape from the difficulties here in question [1] may be useful at this point, for it is a common observation that those who lack experience find a general discussion of this subject troublesome. We may, therefore, consider a well known physico-chemical system comprising a liquid and a gas phase. The liquid phase is an aqueous solution of carbonic acid, sodium bicarbonate, and two salts of phosphoric acid: monosodium phosphate and disodium phosphate. The gas phase contains carbon dioxide. For convenience, we consider that this carbon dioxide on entering the liquid phase at once becomes carbonic acid. This system may be regarded as made up of the four components, water, carbon dioxide, phosphoric acid, and sodium hydroxide, since a mixture of these substances in suitable amounts

[1] See above, p. 13.

will constitute the system. To a first approximation the concentration of water is constant. Therefore we neglect this component. A chemical reaction occurs in the liquid phase; for our present purposes it may be written as follows:

$$H_2CO_3 + Na_2HPO_4 \rightleftharpoons NaHCO_3 + NaH_2PO_4.$$

If we designate the concentrations of these four substances by the symbols $[H_2CO_3]$, $[Na_2HPO_4]$, $[NaHCO_3]$, and $[NaH_2PO_4]$, which are to be treated like four algebraical quantities, we may represent the experimentally determined conditions for the chemical equilibrium as follows:

$$\frac{[H_2CO_3] \times [Na_2HPO_4]}{[NaHCO_3] \times [NaH_2PO_4]} = \frac{1}{3} \tag{1}$$

There is also a physical equilibrium between carbon dioxide in the gas phase and free carbonic acid in the liquid phase. If we designate the concentration of carbon dioxide in the gas phase by $[CO_2]_G$, the experimentally determined conditions for this equilibrium are given by the equation:

$$[CO_2]_G = [H_2CO_3]. \tag{2}$$

Here the condition of equilibrium is conceived as that state in which the velocity of a process in one direction is equal to the velocity in the opposite direction, so that there is no net change and therefore no observable change in the composition of the system. We shall assume a constant temperature and neglect all other considerations, in a first approximation. This is essential in order to attain the greatest possible simplicity of illustration. But the reader must not suppose that the description of this system is more than a very rough representation of the facts, or that it takes into account the modern theories of solution. It is obtained by means of a method of mathematical analysis different from that of Gibbs and easier to understand.

In such a system let the volume of each phase be 1 liter and let the concentrations, expressed in arbitrary units, have the following values:

$$[CO_2]_G \quad = \quad 1.0,$$
$$[H_2CO_3] \quad = \quad 1.0,$$
$$[NaHCO_3] = \quad 10.0,$$
$$[NaH_2PO_4] = \quad 30.0,$$
$$[Na_2HPO_4] = 100.0.$$

Then reference to equations (1) and (2) shows that equilibrium exists.

Since the volumes of the two phases are equal, the concentrations are measures of the masses of the substances, expressed in terms of chemical equivalents, for mass is equal to concentration multiplied by volume.

Let us now suppose that carbon dioxide is introduced into the gas phase in amount sufficient to raise the value of $[CO_2]_G$ instantaneously to 101.0; that is to say, let the added mass of carbon dioxide be equal to 100.0 in the present units. In this manner, the physical equilibrium between carbon dioxide in the gas phase and free carbonic acid in the liquid phase will be disturbed and carbon dioxide will move into the liquid phase. This, in turn, will disturb the chemical equilibrium in the liquid phase, and the reaction represented above will run from left to right. We now require a quantitative description of the state of equilibrium that will be finally reached.

In addition to equations (1) and (2) we have the following further information concerning the masses of the components: First,

$$[CO_2]_G + [H_2CO_3] + [NaHCO_3] = 112.0, \quad (3)$$

for the total carbon dioxide of the system is represented by the sum of these three quantities and, since their sum was originally 12 units and since 100 units have been added, the total must now be 112 units.

Secondly,

$$[NaH_2PO_4] + [Na_2HPO_4] = 130.0, \quad (4)$$

for all the phosphoric acid of the system is in these two forms, and the amount is unchanged.

Thirdly,

$$[NaHCO_3] + [NaH_2PO_4] + 2[Na_2HPO_4] = 240.0, (5)$$

for all the sodium of the system is in these three forms: one atom of sodium per molecule in each of the two first, two atoms in the third form; and the amount of sodium in the system is unchanged.

We have now five equations, and since five concentrations are in question nothing more remains but the algebraical solution. Equations (3), (4), and (5) give:

$$[NaHCO_3] = 112.0 - 2[H_2CO_3],$$
$$[NaH_2PO_4] = 132.0 - 2[H_2CO_3],$$
$$[Na_2HPO_4] = -2.0 + 2[H_2CO_3].$$

Substituting these values in equation (1) we find:

$$\frac{[H_2CO_3] \times \{-2 + 2[H_2CO_3]\}}{\{112 - 2[H_2CO_3]\} \times \{132 - 2[H_2CO_3]\}} = \frac{1}{3}.$$

The solution of this equation is: $[H_2CO_3] = 27.5$ approximately. Therefore,

$$[CO_2]_G \quad = 27.5,$$
$$[NaHCO_3] = 57.0,$$
$$[NaH_2PO_4] = 77.0,$$
$$[Na_2HPO_4] = 53.0,$$

and these values satisfy all five equations.

The amount of carbon dioxide that has moved from the gas to the liquid phase is $101.0 - 27.5 = 73.5$ units. The amount of carbonic acid that has been converted into sodium bicarbonate is $57.0 - 10.0 = 47.0$ units, and an equal quantity of disodium phosphate has been converted into monosodium phosphate.

For the reader who is unfamiliar with chemistry the following algebraical formulation of the above discussion may be useful.   Let

$[CO_2]_G$ = x = concentration of carbon dioxide in the gas phase.

$[H_2CO_3]$ = y = concentration of free carbonic acid in the liquid phase.

$[NaHCO_3]$ = z = concentration of sodium bicarbonate in the liquid phase.

$[NaH_2PO_4]$ = u = concentration of monosodium phosphate in the liquid phase.

$[Na_2HPO_4]$ = v = concentration of disodium phosphate in the liquid phase.

$[CO_2]_G + [H_2CO_3] + [NaHCO_3] = M_1$ = mass of the component carbon dioxide.

$[NaH_2PO_4] + [Na_2HPO_4] = M_2$ = mass of the component phosphoric acid.

$[NaHCO_3] + [NaH_2PO_4] + 2[Na_2HPO_4] = M_3$ = mass of the component sodium hydroxide.

Then we have the following equations, which are known to hold for the system:

$$\frac{y\,v}{z\,u} = \frac{1}{3}, \tag{I}$$

$$\frac{x}{y} = 1, \tag{II}$$

$$x + y + z = M_1, \tag{III}$$

$$u + v = M_2, \tag{IV}$$

$$z + u + 2v = M_3. \tag{V}$$

For the first condition of equilibrium we take

$$M_1 = 12.0,\ M_2 = 130.0,\ M_3 = 240.0,$$

and for the second condition of equilibrium we take

$$M'_1 = M_1 + 100.0 = 112.0,\ M'_2 = M_2 = 130.0,$$
$$M'_3 = M_3 = 240.0.$$

We now substitute in turn these two sets of values of the M's in the five equations and solve. These two solutions are given in the following parallel columns.

	First State	Second State
x	1.0	27.5
y	1.0	27.5
z	10.0	57.0
u	30.0	77.0
v	100.0	53.0

In this instance, if equations (1) and (2) were known, reasoning by a sequence of cause and effect would proceed as follows: We first consider the application of equation (2). The value of $[CO_2]_G$ = x is now 101, that of $[H_2CO_3]$ = y is 1. In order

that $[CO_2]_G$ may be equal to $[H_2CO_3]$, 50 units of
carbon dioxide must pass into the solution, for
then $[CO_2]_G = [H_2CO_3] = 51$. But this change
must disturb the chemical equilibrium. Accordingly, we now calculate from equation (1) a new
condition of equilibrium. This is done in a manner
that is similar to the calculation above worked out,
but with the difference that we set the value of
$[H_2CO_3] + [NaHCO_3]$ for the liquid phase at
51 + 10 or 61, thereby assuming that the readjustment of the chemical equilibrium is unmodified by
a simultaneous change in the physical equilibrium,
just as the first stage of the process was conceived
as the attainment of the physical equilibrium between the two phases, through movement of carbon
dioxide, unmodified by a change in this chemical
equilibrium. The result of this second computa-
tion is that of the 51 units of free carbonic acid in
solution a little more than 15 units will be left after
the chemical reaction has run its course. We next
return to equation (2) and note that now $[CO_2]_G +$
$[H_2CO_3] = 51 + 15 = 66$. Thus, in accordance
with our assumptions, we find that a second movement of carbon dioxide into the liquid phase will
lead to a condition of physical equilibrium when

$$[CO_2]_G = [H_2CO_3] = 33,$$

which involves a further movement of 18 units of
carbon dioxide into the liquid phase. We now return to equation (1), then again to equation (2),
and so on indefinitely. In this instance such a procedure will finally lead to a close approximation to
the solution of the problem, i.e. to the results first
worked out above.

In the last analysis all this consideration reduces to the recognition of differences between the processes of solving one equation, two simultaneous equations, three simultaneous equations, etc.

Two things should now be clear: (1) the inconvenience of the use of the second method, because it neglects the simultaneity of interaction between the physical and the chemical processes; (2) the inadequacy of the conceptual scheme of the second method, because it fails to take into account this simultaneity of interaction.

This simple example illustrates logical principles that find almost universal application in the physical, biological, and social sciences. It also points to the fact that mathematical analysis, or alternatively some form of geometrical representation, has been found indispensable for the complete solution of problems whenever such principles are involved. When quantitative data are lacking, the use of mathematical methods is greatly restricted and generally impossible. But the logical principles are no less valid on that account, and they must still be applied. It has been observed again and again that this application, difficult at best without the aid of quantitative data, is impossible for those who lack the experience afforded by the use of mathematics in the solution of similar problems.

NOTE 4

DETERMINACY AND THE PROPERTIES OF SYSTEMS

All conceptual schemes that take the form of 'systems' seem to have certain characteristics in common.[1] These common characteristics depend upon properties of mathematical or, speaking more generally, of logical operations, and for the present they appear to be unavoidable. In many instances they depend in particular upon the logical necessity, or at least the high expediency, of setting up determinate conditions, because real conditions are found to be at least approximately determined. Isolation serves this purpose well. For example, in the case of physico-chemical systems, isolation, together with the facts that are expressed by some of the widest inductions from experience, like the principles of the conservation of mass and of energy, enables us to write certain equations. Thus equations (I) and (II) of the preceding note, which hold only for a particular constant temperature, depend upon isolation for their validity, because this prevents indeterminate variation of temperature. Similarly equations (III), (IV), and (V), which define the masses of the components, may be used because isolation prevents variation of these masses. In this case, if the system were not isolated, carbon dioxide would escape into the air. An analogous advantage is obtained by the use in theoretical mechanics of the fiction of conservative forces and in thermodynamics of the fiction of reversible cycles.

Isolation may be regarded as the case where exchanges between the system and the environment have the value 0. If these exchanges have some other known value, the requirements for logical analysis are likewise fulfilled, and the analysis may

[1] See above, p. 16.

not present any serious inconvenience. Thus a metal bar one end of which is being heated at a constant rate, or a country with a constant immigration rate, may for certain purposes be treated as a system, without regard to the properties of the source of heat, or of the countries from which the immigrants come.

When actual systems are in fact nearly isolated, the task of the investigator is greatly facilitated and simplified. Kepler had this good fortune in formulating his three laws, and Newton enjoyed the same advantage in elaborating the principles of celestial mechanics. But it must not be supposed that a close approximation to isolation, or even constant exchange, is a necessary condition for the successful approximate description of concrete systems. With the help of estimates of disturbances introduced from without and of other disturbances that result from actions in the opposite direction, even when such disturbances are very complex, much can often be accomplished when the characteristics of the ideal isolated system are known.

Pareto's social system conforms to these logical principles. His conceptual scheme is an ideal system and isolated. His treatment of actual concrete systems aims to take account of the difficulties that depend upon lack of isolation.

In order that the conditions in a system shall be determined, or even partially understood, it is necessary to choose certain variables and to obtain information about the mathematical functions by which the relations between these variables may be represented and which describe the system, or alternatively to do one's best with qualitative data, bearing in mind the results of three centuries of experience with applied mathematics, or, in other words, bearing in mind the relevant logical principles.

The choice of variables or definitions, and therefore of concepts, is very important in beginning the systematic treatment of a new subject. It may be almost intuitive, as in the beginnings of mechanics, or nearly obvious as the result of a long period of scientific development, as in the case of Gibbs's physico-chemical system, or a difficult task demanding long preliminary consideration, as in the case of Pareto's social system. Only experience can judge the adequacy of Pareto's choice.

To think in words about many things simultaneously is impossible. To deal with many variables in mathematical work is likely to be excessively inconvenient. Therefore, it is desirable that the classes of variables should not be too numerous. For the logical analysis, the fewer they are, the better. This is why Gibbs eliminated capillary and electrical phenomena and the effect of gravity from the first part of his work on heterogeneous equilibrium, when he defined his system. Pareto also takes pains to reduce the number of classes of variables to a minimum. On the other hand, his social system is the result of increasing the number of classes of variables of his economic system, when the facts made this necessary.

The choice of variables, as a result of some process of analysis and abstraction, is followed or, as often happens, preceded by their description, and by the discovery of relations between them. These relations may be of a very general character, like Newton's three laws of motion, or the laws of conservation, or the second law of thermodynamics, and in these cases confusion may arise between description and definition; [1] or they may be more specific, like the properties of carbon dioxide set down in the preceding note; or they may be properties of a particular system, like the mass of phosphoric acid in the particular system there considered, or the mass of the sun. A great part of Pareto's book is devoted to descriptions of his variables and to discussion of the relations between them.

Another characteristic of many ideal systems that is, in general, indispensable in order that conditions shall be determinate is the establishment and use of some definition of equilibrium or some criterion of equilibrium, whether in the case of statical equilibrium or in the case of dynamical equilibrium. For the abstract conceptual scheme this is as a rule the decisive feature that goes farthest to establish determinate conditions. This criterion is often of such a character that some function like entropy or energy assumes a maximum or a minimum value or, as in the case of the derivatives or variations of such functions, vanishes. In the case of Pareto's social system the definition of equilibrium takes a form that closely resembles the theorem of Le Chatelier in physical chemistry,

[1] See V. F. Lenzen, *The Nature of Physical Theory*, New York, 1931, passim.

which expresses a property of physico-chemical equilibrium, and which may be deduced from the work of Gibbs.

In any event the aim of all this is to make possible the formulation of a set of equations, like equations (I), (II), (III), (IV), and (V) of the preceding note, in number equal to the number of variables, and such that all the conditions may be determined. Moreover, since it is desirable to do this for as many concrete instances as possible, every effort is made to discover the general properties of the systems in question and to formulate these properties so that they may be used in each concrete instance.

Here Pareto's social system fails to reach its goal, and no doubt it will be long before this goal can be reached. Yet, partial successes may be credited to Pareto's effort even here, for he has described not a few general properties of the social system. But the prospect of the introduction of quantitative methods in sociology, in such a manner as is necessary for the mathematical description of a social system, seems remote indeed. However, the logical conditions for determinacy remain, and they point toward a single path. This is the path that Pareto has chosen.

The interdependence of the variables in a system is one of the widest inductions from experience that we possess; or we may alternatively regard it as the definition of a system. It also finds its formulation in the mathematical description of all kinds of systems.

Finally, we may distinguish a fact that probably

depends on psychological rather than logical characteristics of thought. Many systems, including the social system, contain 'objects'; these objects have 'properties' and 'relations' and they are 'moved' by 'forces.' Thus our kinesthetic needs find expression as they did in the discrimination of primary and secondary qualities and in Lord Kelvin's requirement of a model as an almost indispensable aid to the understanding of physical phenomena.

It will be convenient to consider all this more explicitly with the help of our illustration of the preceding note. Let us write, instead of equations (I) and (II), the equations:

$$\frac{y\,v}{z\,u} = k_1, \tag{A}$$

$$\frac{x}{y} = k_2. \tag{B}$$

These are the expressions of two general laws of physical chemistry. They hold approximately for any chemical reaction of the form $A + B = C + D$ and for the distribution of any substance between two phases, respectively. The equations,

$$k_1 = \frac{1}{3},$$

$$k_2 = 1,$$

by means of which equations (I) and (II) may be derived from equations (A) and (B), express experimental results of measurements of the properties of the chemical substances in question. They hold for any system that contains these substances, if the implied conditions of temperature, etc., are fulfilled.

Similarly we may write an equation:

$$am_1 + bm_2 + cm_3 + \ldots = M. \qquad (C)$$

This equation is the statement of the law of the conservation of mass. In conformity with this principle, equation (III),

$$x + y + z = M_1,$$

states the facts about the mass of the component carbon dioxide for the class of systems in question, equation (IV) similarly states the facts regarding the mass of the component phosphoric acid, and equation (V) the facts regarding the mass of the component sodium hydroxide, for the same class of systems. Here M_1, M_2, and M_3 are total masses, corresponding to the M of equation (C), and x, y, z, u, and v represent the m's of that equation. The values of a, b, c . . . of equation (C) are all equal to 1 in equations (III), (IV), and (V), except in the third term of equation (V), where the value is 2.

It must be carefully noted that x, y, z, u, and v represent both masses and concentrations because, for convenience of exposition, the conditions have been so set up. Otherwise, equations (III), (IV), and (V) would be a little more complicated in accordance with the fact that mass = concentration x volume, which is a definition.

Finally, when we put numbers in place of M_1, M_2, and M_3 we state facts that are descriptive in each instance of a single system.

When all this has been done, we have, for example, the equations:

$$\frac{y}{z}\frac{v}{u} = \frac{1}{3}, \qquad \text{(I)}$$

$$\frac{x}{y} = 1, \qquad \text{(II)}$$

$$x + y + z = 112, \qquad \text{(III}_2\text{)}$$

$$u + v = 130, \qquad \text{(IV}_2\text{)}$$

$$z + u + 2v = 240. \qquad \text{(V}_2\text{)}$$

This system of five simultaneous algebraical equations completely describes and defines, to a particular approximation, in terms of a particular conceptual scheme, a particular physico-chemical system in a state of equilibrium, conformably with the various assumptions of a certain fixed temperature, isolation, etc. that have been made. The accuracy of the description depends upon the accuracy of the inductions that have been employed in the form of the general equations (A), (B), and (C), on the accuracy of the less general statements of the equations (III), (IV), and (V), and on the accuracy of the measurements that give rise to the various numbers of the five equations (I), (II), (III$_2$), (IV$_2$), and (V$_2$).

In this case the definition of equilibrium, which may be employed in setting up equations (A) and (B) and which is therefore implied in equations (I) and (II), is that equilibrium is that state where the velocity of a process running in one direction is equal to the velocity of the process running in the opposite direction. Let us consider equation (II), which defines the equilibrium between carbon dioxide in the gas phase and free carbonic acid in the liquid phase.

Here the facts concerning velocity are expressed by two equations,

$$V_G = K_G x,$$
$$V_L = K_L y,$$

where V_G and V_L represent the rate of entrance of gas into the liquid phase and the rate of escape of gas from the liquid phase respectively, and K_G and K_L are constants.

When $V_G = V_L$, we find:

$$K_G x = K_L y,$$

$$\text{and} \quad \frac{x}{y} = \frac{K_L}{K_G}.$$

Then it is evident from equation (II) that

$$\frac{K_L}{K_G} = 1,$$

which is another statement of the results of experiment.

The definition of equilibrium here employed is, for scientific purposes, inferior to Gibbs's thermo-dynamical definition. I have made use of it and of the whole present explanation because of its great simplicity, for the benefit of those who are not familiar with mathematics, in spite of the fact that it does not fully illustrate the properties of Gibbs's conceptual scheme.

NOTE 5

THE SOURCES OF PARETO'S SOCIAL SYSTEM

Here [1] I mean to imply that: (1) The characteristics of physico-chemical phenomena have nothing to do directly with the characteristics of Pareto's conceptual scheme. In other words the social system is not the result of the application of the *facts* of physics and chemistry to sociology.

(2) It is very unlikely that the general characteristics of Gibbs's system had anything to do with Pareto's construction of his social system. In other words, it is very probable, I think nearly certain, that Pareto did not keep Gibbs's work in mind and *a fortiori* that he did not imitate it, when he worked out his social system; so that Pareto's system is not the result of the application of the *theories* of physical chemistry to sociology.

(3) It is still more unlikely that the specific characteristics of Gibbs's system that I have used as analogies for the purpose of illustration influenced Pareto's construction of his social system. In this sense the analogies that I have pointed out are accidental. In other words Gibbs's system is almost certainly not a source of Pareto's system.

Then what is the explanation of these analogies? I think it may be found in the consideration set out above in Note 4.

Let us compare the solar system, the physico-chemical system, and the social system. The sun, planets, asteroids, and moons are analogous to Gibbs's components or to Pareto's individuals.

[1] See above, p. 17.

The groups of these bodies, each consisting of a planet with its dependent moons, roughly correspond to the phases of physical chemistry and to Pareto's social heterogeneity. Mass and motion in celestial mechanics; concentrations, temperature, and pressure in physical chemistry; the manifestations of sentiments, verbal elaborations, and the economic interests in sociology are likewise analogous. Finally force, entropy, and the sentiments are convenient theories or conventions that find application in mechanics, in thermodynamics, and in sociology, respectively.

Now these rough analogies seem to be due in some measure to very general psychological properties of thought like that referred to in the last paragraph of the preceding note. They also depend upon the logical limitations that have been imposed and the logical operations that have been developed during three centuries of evolution of applied mathematics. These are the principal topics of the preceding note and I shall not further discuss them.

The early sources of Pareto's theory may, therefore, be sought in the works of Galileo, Kepler, Huygens and Newton, of Euler and Lagrange; the late sources are to be found in the mathematical economics of Walras and Pareto's own extension of that work during the early years of his professorship at Lausanne.

While yet a student in the Polytechnic School of Turin, Pareto wrote a thesis on the mathematical theory of equilibrium in elastic solids. At that time this subject was fully developed as a department of classical dynamics, and it involved, explicitly or implicitly, all the strictly mathematical principles and most of the logical principles with which we have been concerned. Therefore, it seems probable that this experience, which is so closely related to what came after it, helped to determine the whole course of Pareto's intellectual development. He must have acquired at that early stage much of the necessary skill and much of the necessary understanding that enabled him to do his later work.

Pareto has himself described how his sociology grew out of his economics, and his social system may be precisely defined as the modification of his economic system by the introduction of the variables that he found he could no longer neglect in studying the phenomena. These variables are the manifestations of the sentiments, called by him residues, verbal elaborations, which he calls derivations, and social heterogeneity.

In this note I have tried to show that Pareto's work is both intrinsically and through its origins in the classical tradition; that it seems to be the result of his own private intellectual development over many years; and that it resembles the work of others in other fields chiefly because, like the work of these others, it conforms to the tested and proved requirements of logic and mathematics.

NOTE 6

THE UTILITY OF PARETO'S SOCIAL SYSTEM

The social system seems, therefore, to bear a relation to all the subjects of the first class similar to that which, at the time of its publication, Gibbs's physico-chemical system bore to chemistry, metallurgy, geology, physiology, and other subjects.[1] Accordingly, we may expect that this conceptual scheme, suitably modified in accordance with experience, will prove useful in the investigation of many of the phenomena with which the subjects of the first class are concerned. No doubt this usefulness may be expected to arise chiefly when description of interrelations of the parts of a particular system, rather than analysis of the parts, is in question; though the importance, deduced from his inductions, that is assigned by Pareto to certain parts and certain factors of a system rather than to others, is not to be despised as a guide in mere analysis. In particular his demonstration of the importance of the residues and of the secondary role of the derivations is widely, indeed all but universally, applicable.

The use of Pareto's social system in the study of the subjects of the first class is desirable and, judging by the experience of other sciences, the application of some such conceptual scheme is indispensable; but the task is not easy. We may note certain obvious difficulties. (1) Among the endless variety of subjects that are included in the social sciences, there may well be more where the consideration of the social system is irrelevant than has been found to be the case in the application of the physico-chemical system to the sciences in which it has been found useful. Here experience

[1] See above, p. 18.

alone can determine the outcome. (2) It seems probable (a) that close approximation to isolation is a less common characteristic of actual social systems than of actual physical and chemical systems, and (b) that arbitrary choice and delimitation of concrete social systems may prove to be more difficult than arbitrary delimitation of concrete physical and chemical systems. (3) The experimental formation of social systems is very difficult. (4) The sharp discrimination and definition of economic interests and of verbal elaborations is more difficult than the definition of such things as concentration, temperature, and pressure in physical chemistry, while the precise characterization of the manifestations of sentiments is perhaps one of the most difficult tasks that can be undertaken. (5) But the greatest restriction upon the use of the social system depends upon the impossibility, at least for the present, of the use of suitable quantitative methods in the study of the phenomena.[1]

For these reasons I think we may say that Pareto's social system is an invaluable conceptual scheme, but that it is now, and will probably long remain, an implement of limited usefulness in the working up of data. This defect, however, seems to reside in the character of the available data and not in the instrument. Those who wish to enjoy the

---

[1] Yet we must not forget a fact that was long ago stated by Cournot: "One of the most important functions of [mathematical] analysis precisely consists in assigning determined relations between quantities whose numerical values, and even algebraical forms, are absolutely unassignable." Trans. from *Théorie des Richesses*, Paris, 1838, p. 51. See, for a more extensive quotation and a discussion, F. Y. Edgeworth, *Mathematical Psychics*, London, 1881, pp. 83, 84.

conveniences that the physical sciences afford must still cleave to the physical sciences.

NOTE 7

PARETO'S USE OF HIS SOCIAL SYSTEM

It is an interesting and probably unanswerable question how far Pareto was clearly aware of the position of the social system in his book.[1] Needless to say, he knew what he was doing. But it is possible that he knew it so well that, aside from his use of the theory of equilibrium, he was not clearly aware of it. As I have tried to explain, the logical principles, the methods, and the point of view are in the main common to the treatment of all systems, in whatever science they may occur, and no alternative procedure is known, none at least that will bear logical criticism. From his youth Pareto had been familiar with all this and he had used first dynamical systems and then for many years the economic system in his daily work. Thus, it must all have become habitual, and so it may have become in a manner unconscious.

Throughout the Treatise, Pareto has much to say about scientific method, and, if I may judge from my own experience, I know no more useful statement of its necessary and sufficient characteristics. But in this connection he says little or nothing about systems. Moreover, the discussion of this subject has also been similarly overlooked by others. Indeed, I am acquainted with no satisfactory treatment of it and with few that go even as

[1] See above, p. 20.

far as the very inadequate discussion that I have written in the present Essay.

The answer to the question raised in this note is probably not very important. But the fact that it seems not unreasonable to pose the question is a significant indication of Pareto's acquired skill in performing the task that he had undertaken. And finally the consideration of the question suggests an explanation of some of the difficulties of the work. For there are passages in the Treatise that are troublesome to many readers, but clear to those who approach the subject with an experience similar to that of the author. In order that one may overlook a thing because it is so familiar that one does not notice it, a necessary condition is that it should be so familiar.

NOTE 8

NON-LOGICAL ACTIONS

Pareto has probably made use of the term non-logical [1] with more than one meaning. From the point of view adopted in the present Essay the question raised by this criticism is not very important, as I shall now try to show. The discussion will enable me to describe more completely certain features of the work.

In Chapter II of the Treatise Pareto studies non-logical actions. He begins by noting that the direct consequence of an action may be considered in two aspects: first, as it really is and, secondly, as it appears to certain men. Some distinction of this kind

[1] See above, p. 20.

is necessary in order to classify separately such operations as those of a chemist on the one hand and those of a magician on the other. Next he defines the terms objective and subjective. The aspect of things and events as they really are, or, speaking more carefully, as the most complete available knowledge of the facts represents them, is objective. The aspect of things and events as they appear to a particular individual is subjective. These two aspects may be approximately identical, or more or less different, or altogether unlike. Pareto then defines logical actions as actions of which the anticipated direct consequences are [probably] objectively and subjectively identical [to a first approximation]. Here I have introduced in square brackets the limitations upon the definition that Pareto again and again insists upon as invariably implicit in all his statements of fact, inductions and even deductions. All other actions are non-logical. It should be noted that either or both consequences may be absent. In these cases, the action is non-logical.[1] From the scientific standpoint this definition seems to involve but one difficulty, namely that of determining subjective consequences, i.e. the results that a man expects from his actions.

[1] The relative importance of logical and of non-logical actions in a social system is a quantitative problem that I have not discussed in this Essay. The reader should, therefore, take note of the risk of underestimating the importance of logical actions merely because they are not here discussed. As a result of the earlier development of economics and in view of the role of logical actions in the economic system, these actions are, in a rough approximation, treated by Pareto as a rule only in their relation to the interests.

Experience shows that a sociology from which the study of subjective consequences is excluded is an inconveniently restricted science. A good inductive proof of this conclusion may be observed in the importance of intent in law. Further evidence may be found in such works as Caesar's *Commentaries*, Machiavelli's *Prince* and *Discourses*, Chesterfield's *Letters*, or in any treatise on such various subjects as strategy, politics, or business policy. Pareto's position is that in the case of magical operations, of sacrifices to the gods, of sorcery, and many others of like nature, no less than in the operations of engineering or of manufacture, the facts are often sufficient to determine subjective consequences.

A study of facts follows. This leads to the demonstration that non-logical actions, that is to say, actions that are not what Pareto has defined as logical actions, are both very common and very important social phenomena. I think there can be no doubt that the demonstration is unexceptionable and conclusive, and that the theorem cannot be forgotten with impunity.

This stage of Pareto's progress is followed by a chapter on non-logical actions in the history of doctrines, by another on theories that go beyond experience, and by a third on pseudo-scientific theories. Here, as in the chapter on non-logical actions, he proceeds inductively, studying a multitude of facts and slowly pressing forward toward the discrimination of residues, or manifestations of the sentiments, and derivations, or verbal elaborations.

For the purpose of analysis and as an aid in

building up the characterization of the social system, non-logical actions have now done their work. They are of no further importance in Pareto's reasoning. At most they serve the purpose of passing reference or illustration. Moreover, not only everything that follows the recognition of residues and derivations but also all that precedes and leads up to them may be founded upon the use of these terms without the use of the term non-logical action. Thus the term non-logical action is seen to be a part of the scaffolding by means of which Pareto constructs his definitive logical structure.

Therefore, the question of inconsistency in the use of the word non-logical is of secondary importance, because, if I am not mistaken: (1) Pareto has fully demonstrated the existence and importance of non-logical actions, as clearly defined by him in Chapter II. (2) This unexceptionable portion of his work is entirely sufficient, with the help of his great array of facts, to establish his residues and derivations. (3) Once established, the residues and derivations replace the non-logical actions, not only in the later portions of the work, but, by a rigorous implication of the definition of the social system, in the whole book, as the logical foundation of all the theories.

I shall not undertake a discussion in detail of this question of inconsistency in the use of the word non-logical. No experienced person will doubt that Pareto has frequently fallen into inconsistencies of this kind in writing a book of nearly a million words, especially on such a subject. But I venture to say that there are not a few examples of apparent inconsistencies in the Treatise that depend upon Pareto's failure to point out facts or considerations that he knew very well indeed, that he had in mind, but that had to be pointed out to make a correct statement logically complete.

The natural expression in words of clear thinking is elliptical, and it is often the more elliptical, the more persistent, continuous, and methodical the thought, when the thought is greatly concerned with things, operations, and events, and not merely with words and ideas. Those whose experience is mainly with observation and experiment and scientific theories more easily grasp the elliptically expressed thought and the facts behind it, and are less likely to be confused; those whose experience is more largely with words and ideas have greater difficulty. This explains some of the difficulties with Pareto's use of the term non-logical.

I think there are probably other difficulties. In so far as they are due to real inconsistency in the use of the term non-logical, I suggest that they are probably for the most part the result of a careless use of words by Pareto while he was thinking about things. This is another familiar phenomenon. Once again it causes more inconvenience to one class of readers than to another. But, I repeat, whatever difficulties there may be in Pareto's use of the term non-logical, they are not of such a nature that the logical structure of his work is sensibly affected by them, nor do they touch the facts that are the foundation of the work.

One more point may be made. Logical and non-logical actions are not separable, like prime and

thinking in words and ideas without a consideration of the relevant facts. Since the defense involves a reference to an important feature of Pareto's work, it will be useful to state it succinctly.

It should be noted that: (1) Pareto carefully abstains from the argument from analogy. He often uses analogy, but only as a means of illustration. (2) This particular analogy is badly chosen, in so far as it fails, in some instances or for some readers, to illustrate the subject in question. Let us, therefore, consider another analogy that may possibly serve the purpose more successfully. Galileo analyzed the parabolic motion of a projectile into uniform motion in a straight line and uniformly accelerated motion downward, and this has proved to be a decisive step in the history of science. Here the analysis, like Pareto's, is logical or mental, and it is obviously not physical. Huygens, Newton, and all later physicists have followed the example of Galileo.

We may now consider a closer analogy. And this time we choose from chemistry an example that does not involve either physical or chemical separation of parts. Glycocoll or aminoacetic acid is represented by the symbol $NH_2 - CH_2 - COOH$. It is a substance that forms compounds with both acids and bases. Combination with an acid is, by abstraction, attributed to the NH_2-radical, combination with a base to the $COOH$-radical. But in a closer approximation the combination with acid is conceived as modified by the presence of the $COOH$-radical and the combination with base as modified by the presence of the NH_2-radical.

One might go on with the consideration of examples from all the other sciences and thus reach a familiar induction, for an induction is the statement of the existence of a uniformity, and many analogies of the same kind constitute a uniformity. All this is so well known that nothing but ignorance of the facts, or failure to think in terms of the facts, could lead anyone to take the present objection seriously.

It is one of the most general characteristics of the sciences that they proceed by means of abstraction and analysis, and that this is followed by synthesis. Abstract analysis and synthesis, alike, are greatly complicated by the mutual dependence and interaction of the parts, as in the case of glycocoll above noted, as in the field of sociology, and very generally in all the sciences. This is explained at great length, with scrupulous attention to detail and with many illustrations, by Pareto in one of the most successful expositions of the subject that I know. Probably his choice of the composition of a rock as an analogy in a particular instance was due to carelessness and familiarity with his subject, leading to something that falls short of the closest analogy, and therefore of the best illustration.

NOTE 10

CLASSIFICATION

The arrangement of residues in six consecutive classes is an excessively simple classification. For this reason the use of the classification is often unsatisfactory.[1] Little as we know about this subject, it seems practically certain that some highly detailed classification in several dimensions — the classification of organic compounds in chemistry may be cited as an illustration of what I have in mind — will become necessary. This is suggested by the following facts: (1) The first and second classes of residues seem to occupy a peculiar position when the classification is examined from a psychological point of view. Thus the existence of some sort of hierarchy, even in this simple classification, is implied. (2) It is often difficult or impossible to decide in which of two or more classes a given residue should be placed, and this is sometimes not a result of vagueness of definition. On the contrary, it often depends upon the existence of good reasons for each choice. Thus the need of taking account simultaneously of several different kinds of resemblances is implied. (3) The phenomena are very numerous, various, and complex.

It is also probable that a classification, serviceable for the purpose of the sociologist, may prove to be unsatisfactory in some respects for the purposes of the psychologist, or the historian of religions, or the lawyer.

A further difficulty depends upon the fact that we are obliged to make use of our common-sense knowledge of sentiments in classifying their manifestations. Indeed this inconvenience is involved both in diagnosis and in classification. Now such common-sense knowledge is, I think, in some re-

[1] See above, p. 34.

spects more trustworthy for the purpose than certain results of modern psychology might lead us to think. This seems to depend upon the fact that if we use the sentiments only as theories and with due skepticism, and otherwise keep to the *manifestations* of sentiments, which are phenomena, and continually verify by means of them, we can, in the long run, inductively overcome some of the difficulties, because a theory that remains consistent with the facts is harmless to the skilled workman. But one difficulty seems to be intrinsic and inescapable, for our analysis of sentiments, perhaps even more than our analysis of most other experiences, is seldom sharp and detailed, and it is probably never even approximately exhaustive. The history of introspective psychology proves the truth of this statement. Moreover, we often find sentiments inextricably and significantly entangled in aggregates, and these aggregates also have no sharp boundaries.

After all this has been said, however, it seems that Pareto did well to set up a simple classification of the residues, for this conforms to the customary scientific procedure, and a satisfactory classification can hardly be imagined without a foundation constituted by a large amount of work that has been performed with the aid of a sound method and a provisional scheme of classification. As an illustration of what has been necessary elsewhere, let us consider another science. The present knowledge of organic chemistry is the accumulated result of countless experimental researches, the equivalent of the work of not less than two or three thousand intelligent and highly skilled specialists working with perfected methods for a lifetime. In the beginning the classification of organic compounds was very simple and inadequate. It is today perhaps the most complex and elaborate classification that exists, and it has reached this condition by a long process of evolution through adaptations to the facts. Social scientists are prone to overlook such considerations. Yet, there is no reason to doubt that the necessary conditions for the development of any science that deals with complex material are similar. Among these conditions we may recognize (1) an immense amount of methodical, systematic, skilled labor and (2) the use of theories and classifications. The theories are at first crude and the classifications simple, but by adaptation to the facts the theories are refined and the classifications made complex.

Discussions of scientific method are commonly the result of experience in the study of physics and, in lesser degree, of experimental biology. If those who have cultivated physics and physiology had remained silent while those who have become proficient in organic chemistry, in taxonomy, and in nosology had reported their experiences and analyzed them, our knowledge of scientific method would be different from what it is. Probably it would then be less satisfactory, but in any case its general aspect would be singularly different. For instead of systems, classifications would take the first place in our description of the conceptual schemes of men of science, the importance of the difficult art of diagnosis would receive due recogni-

tion, and this note would be as trite as a superficial
description of the method of Archimedes.

Many recent works on the philosophical interpretation of science, written under the influence of
the results of physical research in the present century, fail to take account of the well known but
undescribed experiences of those who study the
most complex phenomena. But in sociology these
experiences also must be exploited, if sociology is
to take full advantage of the successes and failures
of the other sciences. There is no more one-sided
notion, no more extravagant derivation, than that
what is not applied mathematics is not science.
Indeed the conceptual schemes that we call systems and those that we call classifications are in
their proper places alike indispensable as aids in
ordering and representing our experience, and a
preference for one or the other is evidently based
upon an arbitrarily chosen norm or perhaps upon
insufficient experience. From our present point of
view it is, therefore, irrelevant; but we must not
fail to note that the emphasis upon the importance
of mathematics that now widely prevails may be
misleading to sociologists. In order to make use of
variables, definitions are necessary, and when the
facts are very complex, classification is necessary
for definition. Thus, where complex classification
is necessary, some provisional classification must,
in general, precede the use of mathematics, or even
of the kind of logic that the experience of applied
mathematics has taught. This is almost intuitively
perceived by those who set to work seriously on
the facts, but it is not so plain to the onlookers.

NOTE 11

EQUILIBRIUM

A brief discussion may help to explain these statements and to conclude our consideration of systems.[1]

The first step in building up the conceptual scheme of a new generalized system is the recognition, by induction, of a sufficiently definite class of phenomena like those classes designated by the terms dynamical system, physico-chemical system, and economic system. This is followed by the discrimination, definition, and choice of the abstract entities, like components, temperature, and pressure, that suffice for the characterization (to a certain approximation) of the system. This choice is limited by observation and experiment; it is determined by observation, experiment, logical and mathematical considerations, and by convenience. The closer the approximation that is sought, the greater, in general, will be the number of abstract entities that must be accounted for. Moreover, if the treatment is to be mathematical, it is necessary to set up mathematical functions or indices like concentrations in chemical equivalents per liter, temperature on the absolute scale, or pressure in atmospheres, corresponding to the chosen abstract entities.

Let us now suppose that, for a particular class of systems, n of these abstract entities are to be taken into account. Then, there will be n indices involved and therefore n variables. Therefore, also, for the

[1] See above, p. 46.

complete description of the class, n appropriate
equations are necessary; and, for the complete description of a particular system, n equations that
contain in addition to n variables only numbers
(constants) are necessary. The assumption that a
system is determinate to the desired approximation is equivalent to the assumption that, aside
from practical difficulties, these n equations can be
found, or, alternatively, that the facts can be represented graphically or by means of tables.

The finding of the equations for the class of systems is the discovery of general laws (uniformities)
that are descriptive of the class of systems, and the
appropriate application of these laws in the form of
equations. In the case of a particular concrete
system, numerical values, for example a particular
mass, concentration, or temperature or the numerical value of some other particular constant (param-
eter), have to be introduced. Such equations are
commonly spoken of as the conditions. In the more
advanced sciences the most general conditions are
likely to be expressed in the form of differential
equations.

For the complete description of the conditions by
means of equations, the results of counting or of
measurement are indispensable. Therefore, it may
be impossible to set up the equations. But it is evident that this does not affect the logic.

Following one of Newton's rules of reasoning, we
may provisionally assume that systems in general,
whether or not the conditions are known, have the
characteristics that are deducible from the general
mathematical properties of such sets of simul-

taneous equations as are known to describe similar systems and in which the number of variables is equal to the number of equations. One such property is that if one of the variables is *slightly* varied (as the value of the quantity representing the mass of carbon dioxide was *greatly* varied in the discussion of a system in Note 3) then, in general, the solution of the set of equations thus modified has certain properties relatively to the solution of the unvaried set of equations. These are of such a character that, when the set of equations is conceived as representing a concrete system, the result may be interpreted by the statement that if a small modification of the state of the system is imposed upon it, a reaction will take place and this will tend toward the condition that would have existed if the variation had not occurred, very slightly modified by the experience. Moreover, as I have said, experience confirms this conclusion for social systems, and ultimately this is the justification of the procedure.

The set of equations of Note 3 describes a condition of statical equilibrium. The equilibrium is not statical when time enters, either explicitly or implicitly, as a variable in the equations. Such is the case of the solar system or of an economic system, and such must be the general case of a social system. In this event the state of the system varies with time. But this difference is beside the present point, and has no bearing upon the considerations of the preceding paragraph. However, the difference is in other respects a striking one, and for this reason, it is well to bear in mind that in Pareto's

Treatise equilibrium is a technical term and that its meaning is just that stated in his definition, neither more nor less.

It is unfortunate that the term equilibrium is used in different senses in different sciences. I think the present state of affairs may be made clear by considering the meaning of the term in mechanics. In this science it was introduced by Archimedes to describe statical equilibrium and it is still customary to restrict the use of the term to this case. But an indication that it is possible, and the implication that it may be convenient, to extend the use of the term to dynamics can be stated very easily, as follows: The fundamental principle of dynamics may be represented by the equation [1]

$$\sum \left\{ \left(X - \frac{dI_x}{dt}\right) \delta x + \left(Y - \frac{dI_y}{dt}\right) \delta y + \left(Z - \frac{dI_z}{dt}\right) \delta z \right\} = 0$$

Now in the case of translatory motion or rest when the momentum of each particle is constant, the terms containing dt (t = time) drop out, and this equation reduces to the equation

$$\Sigma(X\delta x + Y\delta y + Z\delta z) = 0$$

which states the principle of virtual displacements and which may be regarded as the fundamental equation of statics because all the conditions of statical equilibrium in all special cases can be deduced from it and the special properties of the

---

[1] V. F. Lenzen, *The Nature of Physical Theory*, New York, 1931, p. 115.

special cases. Thus, it is possible to regard statical equilibrium as a sub-class of the more general condition represented by the more general equation, and it may be convenient even in mechanics to extend the use of the term equilibrium at least to certain other sub-classes of the more general case as, for instance, in the case of translatory or of periodic motion of the system. To do so is to proceed in a manner analogous to that followed by mathematicians in extending the definition of the word number from integers to rational numbers, to irrational numbers, to negative numbers, to imaginary numbers, to transcendent numbers, etc.

In this and the preceding notes I have proceeded from the more concrete to the more abstract logical problems. I shall now try to sum up. Phenomena are regarded as determinate. They are such that uniformities can be recognized. These statements are perhaps our widest inductions from experience. Now the determination by means of general principles of any particular concrete phenomenon to any particular approximation involves the recognition of a certain number of variables. The number of variables that have to be taken into account depends upon the nature of the phenomenon and upon the accuracy of the approximation. Then the determination involves setting up a set of equations, in number equal to the number of variables and of such a character that a unique solution is possible, which express the result of applying the general principles to the particular concrete phenomenon. A state defined by such a set of equations is frequently a state of equilibrium, in the most general sense, conformably with Le Chatelier's theorem and Pareto's definition. The entities designated by the terms of the set of equations, taken together, make up a system. This is a possible definition of the term system. A generalized system is the conceptual scheme which may be obtained by abstraction from a set of concrete systems and which, therefore, enables the investigator to set up the equations for a concrete system.

Finally, it will be convenient to recall the fact that Pareto's social system is the outgrowth, both historically and logically, of his economic system. Logically, it is obtained from the economic system by including in that simpler system the variables that he calls residues, derivations, and social heterogeneity. For this reason his knowledge of the properties of the economic system enabled him to deduce certain other properties of the social system, in addition to those that are properties of systems in general.

NOTE 12

APPLIED SOCIOLOGY

Pareto's grounds for this assertion [1] are worthy of note. Since the social sciences have not arrived at the stage that has been reached by most of the natural sciences, and since it is the presence of strong residues of the first class that lead to the study of all the sciences, social scientists are disposed to reason in terms of derivations from these residues of the first class and from others, which

[1] See above, p. 58.

take the form of what Pareto calls intellectual religions. For this reason in the social sciences derivations predominate over scientific reasoning. Pareto not only saw this in others, but had experienced the difficulty himself, and knew it well as a result of long and arduous efforts to overcome it. Derivations of this kind are commonly more misleading than the opinions of the mere empiricist. For example, before the science of chemistry existed, a common dyer often possessed better judgment than an alchemist, for just these reasons.

Moreover, Pareto notes a marked tendency among social scientists to manifest other sentiments which also give rise to derivations and, upon occasion, to actions that are, in his opinion, unfavorable to the interests of the society in which they live.

Finally, Pareto was firmly convinced from his experience as an economist and sociologist that the time is far distant when it will be, in general, possible to apply the theories of these sciences. For the present he held that trustworthy applications are very few. I think he considered the situation not unlike that of the medical sciences in the seventeenth century.

When derivations are carefully ruled out and plans for the conduct of government or affairs are logically deduced from the well established results of the social sciences, the principal source of error depends upon the fact that by abstraction many factors have been excluded from the considerations that have led to these established results. We have seen that the neglect of factors that can be, for the moment, neglected is a characteristic of all the abstract sciences. But it is easy to forget that factors, both known and unknown, have been neglected, and to suppose, or to assume unconsciously, that logical deductions from well established principles may be applied without modification to practical affairs. In the example of a physico-chemical equilibrium that I have above explained, the effect of variation of temperature is a known factor that was ruled out and it is probable that there are many still unknown factors, even in such a simple phenomenon, that modify the concrete instance.

This is a common source of error and confusion. Pareto has explained it very carefully. Another excellent treatment of the same subject may be found in Whitehead's description [1] of the 'fallacy of misplaced concreteness.' The essential distinction is that between necessary conditions, on the one hand, and necessary *and* sufficient conditions, on the other.

The reader should note very carefully that the validity of a scientific induction is not here in question. What is in question is the degree of abstraction and the applicability of an induction. An induction may be used in describing an event when the factors that have been by abstraction excluded in forming the induction do not interfere with its application to the concrete event. When they do significantly modify the event the induction must be modified by taking these factors into account. Now some factors that are sometimes relevant are

[1] A. N. Whitehead, *Science and the Modern World*, New York, 1926, Chap. III.

always excluded from every induction, for our analysis of experience is never exhaustive. Thus the above considerations hold for all applied science. It should be also noted that the uniform practice of the sciences is not *for these reasons* to reject an induction or a more extensive conceptual scheme, but to modify it. Thus, for instance, Boyle's law, pv = K, becomes, after temperature is accounted for, pv = RT.

NOTE 13

INTERPRETATION OF A DERIVATION

On reconsideration, this phrase, "without undue risk of misunderstanding," [1] seems to me over-optimistic: the expression of a hope that is not in accord with experience. Therefore I feel constrained to set down an interpretation of my derivation, "Pareto's Treatise is a work of genius." It probably implies that the study of the work has been for me a pleasant experience and that I share not only Pareto's conclusions concerning science and method, but also some of his residues, especially those of the first class. After a sustained effort to present a logico-experimental interpretation, I am probably moved not only by a wish to report my experience that the Treatise is useful to many persons doing many different things, but also by a desire, or, speaking ellipitically, by a residue of the third class, to express my sentiments. The derivation does not imply that I believe in the 'existence' of works of genius, for genius, like

[1] See above, p. 59.

Montaigne's "Power, Truth, Justice," is a residue; or that I expect those who dislike Pareto's Treatise or this Essay to be mollified by the derivation; or that I attach to the derivation the slightest intrinsic logico-experimental significance, — except in so far as it may be found illustrative and exemplary.